Western Educational Philosophers

JAGDISH CHAND

Former Deputy Director of Education and
Executive Director of the Delhi Bureau of Textbooks,
Delhi Administration

ANSHAH
Anshah Publishing House

(First Pubished in 2009)

R 75

ISBN: 978-81-8364-093-0

2013 Edition

Western Educational Philosophers

Published by:
ANSHAH PUBLISHING HOUSE
LG, Pankaj Central Market,
IP Ext., Patparganj, Delhi 110092,
Ph.: 91-11-22235152, 9810522367
Br. Off.: 4617/18, Ansari Road,
Delhi -110002

Preface

The book 'Great Philosophers and Thinkers on Education', published in 2006, presents the deeply penetrating and subtle thoughts of the Western and Eastern celebrity masterminds, and includes their publications and contribution to education.

As per the demand in the market and requirement of curriculum in various universities, the book covering Western philosophers on education is brought out independently. It is hoped that this volume will be welcomed by the readers and its advantage is also taken by the pre-service and in-service teachers.

Wide range of primary and secondary sources has been consulted and used for enriching the book, author is grateful to all the authors and their publishers.

Jagdish Chand

Contents

1

Confucius

(551-479 B.C.)

Confucius was ancient China's eminent teacher, philosopher and political theorist. His practical experience and deep thinking have left their mark on educational development not only in China but also in other countries.

Confucius' father, a junior official, died when he was still a child. From a low-grade post of looking after livestock and granaries, he rose through the administrative hierarchy to the post of Minister of Security and Justice for the principality of Lu in one of China's provinces. He devoted his final years in writing and teaching.

Confucius considered that the goal of education was to produce capable individuals whom he called gentlemen or men of quality who combined competence with virtue and whose subsequent careers in administration and government would bring about the ideal of a kingdom managed with integrity.

Education Process

The Great Learning, one of the oldest educational treatises written about 2,500 years ago is attributed to Confucius. In this, he sets out the education process in these words:

> "The Great Learning consists in manifesting the clear character, loving the people and abiding in the highest good... Those who wished to make their wills sincere would first extend their knowledge. The extension of knowledge consists in the investigation of things. When things are investigated, knowledge is extended. When knowledge is extended, the will becomes sincere; when the will is sincere, the mind is rectified; when the mind is rectified, the personal life is cultivated; when the personal life is cultivated, the

family is regulated; when the family is regulated, the state will be in order; and when the state is in order, there will be peace...".

Moral Instruction

Confucius gave a place of pride to moral instruction since what was needed were individuals of outstanding virtue who would assist the rulers in governing with integrity. His ethics, philosophy and politics were inseparable. Virtues emphasised were:

- filial piety
- diligence
- altruism
- affability
- kindness
- frugality
- tolerance
- indulgence
- wisdom and courage
- power of distinguishing what is to be cultivated and what is to be eschewed and
- above all honest and righteous conduct.

According to Confucius all these qualities stem from *'ren'* (humanity or benevolence)

Intellectual Development: Curriculum

Moral instruction did not mean that education should ignore intellectual development of the students. Confucius drafted six manuals for instilling in students the moral values of a feudal society, the basis of an all round culture and the capacities required to exercise official responsibilities. These manuals were:

1. Book of Odes (*'Shi'*).
2. Book of History or Documents (*'Shu'*).
3. The Book of Rites (*'Li'*).
4. The Book of Music (*'Yue'*).
5. The Book of Changes (*'Yi'*).
6. The Spring of Autumn Annals (*'Chungiu'*).

Besides essentially dealing with social relations and ethics, these didactic works also address a number of other subjects including culture, economics, history, philosophy and politics.

The Book of Music has been lost but the five others served for more than 2000 years as the basis of education in feudal China. These manuals were challenged in 1919 by the Violent Fourth May Movement.

Six Arts

Besides the above-mentioned six classics, curriculum also covered the following six arts:

(1) Archery,
(2) Calligraphy,
(3) Chariot-driving,
(4) Mathematics,
(5) Musicianship,
(6) Rites.

Principles of Teaching

In the course of his long career as a teacher, Confucius steadily put together the following laws of pedagogics:

1. Providing students with an education that matched their aptitudes.
2. Inspiring and guiding them and to lead them by stages.
3. Explaining the present in the light of the past.
4. Devoting oneself conscientiously to study and take delight in it.
5. Combining theory with practice.
6. Ensuring that personal behaviour was in conformity with the principles examined.
7. Encouraging independent thought.
8. Taking account of the age of the learners.
9. Practising self-control and analysis.
10. Setting a good example.
11. Correcting one's errors and improving oneself.
12. Curbing evil and exhaling the good.
13. Welcoming criticism.
14. Accepting correction.
15. Forgetting past affronts.

Role of Teachers

Confucius was considered as a remarkable teacher and was revered throughout China. He served as a model for countless generations. He declared, "My teaching is open to everyone, without distinction." In his thirties, he accepted disciples and trained nearly 3,000 of them in his life. The school of Confucius was unique for its age. The ethical code of education which Confucius elaborated and his own performance as a teacher are still considered as his finest and greatest contributions to the cause of learning.

Confucius considered the following qualities as essential for teachers:

1. *Commitment*: A teacher should first and foremost be conscientiously and passionately committed to his work.
2. *Breadth of Knowledge*: His own knowledge must be broad in scope and he should have mastery over it.
3. *Love for Pupils*: For eliciting good results, a teacher must love his pupils.
4. *Understanding of Pupils*: The teacher must know and understand his pupils thoroughly.
5. *Psychological Understanding*: The teacher should understand the psychological peculiarities.
6. *Effective Methodology*: The teacher should develop sound methodology of instruction.
7. *Political Convictions*: The teacher should hold firm political positions.
8. *Human Relations*: The teacher should be modest and discrete in his relations with others.
9. *Expression*: He should convey his knowledge in a disinterested fashion, keeping nothing to himself. He should express elegantly and in a lively fashion.
10. *Moral*: He should cultivate his own personal morality.
11. *Personal Deeds*: He should match his deeds with his words.

Impact on Education

The impact of Confucius has been highlighted by Prof. Yang Huang as:

> "Today, Confucius still has an important place in the education system of countries of the region – Japan, Singapore, the Republic of Korea and Southern Vietnam (before the unification of the country) remained particularly faithful to his thought, especially in the domain of education".

"Although, during his lifetime, Confucius was unable to attain his goals as a teacher, his posthumous contribution to the history of culture and of teaching in China and in other countries throughout the world has won for him not only the reputation of

'Supreme Sage' and 'Teacher of Ten Thousand Generations' in Chinese feudal society, but also what amounts to universal esteem. Since ancient times, many countries have compared their leading scholars, educators and thinkers to Confucius: the distinguished teacher Ch'oe Ch'ung, who opened the first private school in the Kingdom of Koryo, was styled 'the Confucius East of the Sea'; the Enlightenment philosopher Quesnay 'the European Confucius'; the great German poet Goethe 'the Confucius of Weimar'. As a token of the respect and admiration which he inspired, the Italian Jesuit Matteo Ricci, who established parallels between Western and Chinese civilisations, was known as 'the Christian Confucius'.

In China before 1949, his birthday was celebrated as a holiday; this is still the case today in Taiwan, in Vietnam and among the Asian communities of the United States – an occasion marked by commemorative events and ceremonies to honour especially meritorious teachers, and to encourage others to draw inspiration from the virtues of the great educator". (*Prospects*, Vol. 1, 23 (1/2), 1993).

2

Socrates
(469-399 B.C.)

Socrates was born at Athens, Greece, in 469 B.C. His mother was a nurse and father a sculptor. He could not receive any systematic education. It is wondering that without any systematic education, he became one of the greatest philosophers of the world. For sometime he served in the army. Thereafter he started teaching. He wandered and taught. He did not start any educational institution.

Socrates is known for his wisdom and his method of teaching—a kind of dialogue with the students.

Socrates contributed nothing to writing. Our knowledge of him comes from the accounts of some of his pupils, especially Plato. Aristotle was also his disciple.

Socrates was concerned with probing the meaning and truth of ideas by the technique of 'question and answer'. By doing so, he laid the foundations of systematic philosophical thought.

Socrates called into question the institutions of state. He observed,

> "A freeman ought to be a freeman in the acquisition of knowledge. Knowledge which is acquired under compulsion has no hold on mind".

Since Socrates' ideas were not in accord with the rulers. He was charged with corrupting the minds of the youth and condemned to death. He was ordered to take his own life by drinking poison. This was the sad end of Socrates who is still remembered for his wisdom and regarded as one of the greatest philosophers of the world.

Socrates' Philosophy

To Socrates, 'Knowledge is virtue'. The knowledge can be

achieved through knowing oneself. So Socrates said, 'Know thyself'.

He made an intensive study of the works of philosophers and scientists to understand the riddles of life. He came to the conclusion,

> "Love is the hunger of human soul for divine beauty. This beauty is wisdom, virtue, honour, courage, justice and truth. Beauty is truth. And truth is the way that leads directly to God".

He further concluded that the way to the real knowledge, *i.e.,* truth, lay through an intensive study of one's self and the mind of man.

Socratic Method of Instruction: Dialectic Method

Socrates devised a method of analysis and questioning, that is called the Socratic method or approach.

Socratic approach involved at first a generalisation from ordinary experiences and then a definition of the essential idea underlying the particular fact.

Socrates explained his ideas through a process of induction, rather by a process of definition or deduction.

Socrates taught in the open and not in a school.

The aim of the Socratic method was to bring the pupil to the point where he would be able to realise his ignorance and thus acquire the attitude of the true learner. As developed by Socrates, this conversation or quiz method, sometimes called the dialectic method has two stages:

1. The ironic or destructive phase in which, by skilful questioning, the pupil is brought from unconscious ignorance to conscious ignorance.
2. The constructive phase in which, by further questioning, the pupil is led from conscious ignorance to clear and rational truth.

Educational Implications of Socrates' Philosophy

The Socratic method has contributed to the teaching methodology in the following manner:

1. It has given us the inductive approach.

2. Right type of questions are very helpful in leading the learners to the desired goals.
3. Quiz technique is the outcome of the Socratic approach.

Limitations of Socratic Approach

There is always a great danger in this method that it is easier for the teacher to employ the ironic part of the Socratic quiz than the constructive phase. Many teachers lack the ability to use a series of question as a method of developing an understanding of a major concept. There is also the danger that the teacher in his zeal to breakdown unconscious ignorance, may employ sarcasm to an unwholesome extent.

Summing up: The Socratic method can be very effective in overcoming common misconceptions and prejudices, provided it leads, as Socrates would have it, to the consciousness of truth and not merely to the consciousness of ignorance.

3
Plato
(427-347 B.C.)

Rousseau, one of the greatest philosophers of the world, has paid his tribute to Plato in these words:

"If you wish to know what is meant by public education, read Plato's *Republic*. It is the finest treatise on education ever written".

In the words of Emerson, another eminent philosopher:

"Out of Plato come all things that are still written and debated among men of thought".

A.N. Whitehead holds,

"The whole of modern philosophy is a series of footnotes on Plato".

Bertrand Russell states that Plato had a great effect on subsequent ages.

Plato was born in Athens in 427 in a distinguished family. His father was a skilful player. At that time in Greece games were considered as an important medium of educating children. Plato too got his education through these means. Plato read poems and works of Homer (ancient Greek author). However, he could not get his early education properly.

At the age of 20 years, Plato came into contact with Socrates, a great philosopher of his age. There was a lot of economic difference between the two, this did not stand in their way. Socrates was in fact his ideal.

Plato's Visits to Different Countries: After the death of his teacher, Plato was greatly disturbed. He left Athens. With the passage of time, he developed self-confidence and realised his potentialities. He went to Egypt and spent some years there. He engaged himself in search of knowledge. He was greatly influenced by the educational system of Egypt. He went to Italy where he studied the ideas of Pythagoras. He went to Sicily where he studied the administrative system by attending the court of King Dionysus.

Plato's Academy: Plato's philosophy and especially educational and political made a great mark. About 388 B.C., Plato opened his Academy. An academy is the name given to institutions in the field of arts, literature and science. This terms dates back to Plato who began teaching in an olive grove near Athens dedicated to a Greek warrior hero whose name was Academus. Aristotle was one of his students.

Publications

Plato wrote several books, all in the form of a dialogue.

The most important of his classic works are:

1. *Republic*
2. *Laws*

Plato enunciated his views on education in the above mentioned works. These two books provide a lot of knowledge about his educational ideals and programmes.

An Idealist Philosopher

Plato believed that the soul is immortal. Since soul is immortal, it enters into the body even before the child is born. Thus knowledge is present in the child before birth. The process of education should refine this knowledge.

He considered the soul imbibed with virtues.

Wisdom is the eye of the soul. The aim of the life of man is to realise this 'spiritual wisdom'. This wisdom should be awakened through education.

The philosophy of Plato is known as the 'Theory of ideas' or 'Theory of Forms'. This is on account of the fact that he regards the world of ideas above the world of sense perception.

He emphasised the development of qualities of citizenship—Truth, Beauty and Goodness. He considered education as the most important instrument to do this task.

Plato and Education

Meaning of Education

Plato was an idealist and he fully realised the needs of human body and soul. He wrote "Education consists of giving to the body and soul all the perfection of which they are susceptible".

In his book *Laws*, Plato wrote,

> "True education would develop brotherhood. Man is the highest creation. Still he needs education. He will become the most uncivilised living being of earth, if he is not given education".

He elaborated his views further,

> "Education should develop a kind of reason in children in order that they may feel a harmony between the soul and the various things of the world. This harmony is true virtue. Only that education can be regarded good which teaches the child to love that which is good and to hate that is bad".

Plato regarded education as a process of moral training. He wrote,

> "I mean by education that training which is given by suitable habits to the first instincts of virtue in children which leads you always to hate what you ought to hate and love what you ought to love, from the beginning of life to the end".

Morality according to Plato includes truth, control on desire, *i.e.*, self-restraint, intense comprehension, justice, memory and goodness. Justice induces a person for doing noble deeds. Goodness implies human welfare.

Objectives of Education

Following are the main objectives of education according to Plato:

1. Inculcating sentiments of love for truth, beauty and goodness.
2. Harmonising the personality of the child.
3. Producing self-governing individual.
4. Developing a spirit of harmony among children.
5. Developing wisdom.

6. Identifying conflicting elements in life and harmonising them.
7. Harmonising body, mind and soul.
8. Protecting the unity and integrity of the State.
9. Developing civil efficiency.

Education of the Classes: Equipping the three classes of the society, *i.e.,* rulers, soldiers and businessmen, with these qualities which would enable them to discharge their functions effectively. Plato did not feel the necessity of providing education to slaves who formed the fourth class of the society.

Curriculum

Plato was the first educator in the Western world who presented some organisation of the curriculum. Curriculum was envisaged in terms of developing a balanced individual who could lead a balanced life.

Three-fold Division of the Curriculum

(A)	(B)	(C)
Subjects for Physical Development	Subjects for Intellectual Development	Subjects for Aesthetic Development

A. *Physical Development*: It included exercises and gymnastics. Balanced and nourishing diet was also recommended.

B. *Intellectual Development*. This comprised these subjects:

(1) Mathematics,
(2) Geometry,
(3) Philosophy,
(4) Languages,
(5) History,
(6) Polity,
(7) Ethics etc.
(8) Astronomy etc.

C. *Aesthetic Development*. This consisted of Aesthetics (i) Music, (ii) Painting, (iii) Literature Chart showing Stages of Education Subject and Activities

Three-fold Classification of Curriculum—Relating to Three Aspects of Idealism

Truth	*Goodness*	*Beauty*
Intellectual Development	Ethical Development	
(1) Philosophy (2) Logic (3) Mathematics (4) Languages (5) Geography (6) History, Science	(1) Ethics (2) Religion (3) Politics	(1) Art (2) Music (3) Literature (4) Painting

Stages of Education

(1)	(2)	(3)	(4)	(5)	(6)	(7)
Infant stage (1 to 3 years)	Nursery stage (3 to 6 years)	Elementary stage (6 to 13 years)	Secondary stage (13 to 16 years)	Gymnastic stage (16 to 20 years)	Higher Education (20 to 30 years)	Highest Education (30 to 35 years)

Programme of Studies for Each Stage

Sl. No.	*Stage*	*Age Group*	*Subjects/Activities*
1.	Infant stage	From birth to 3 years	Nourishing diet. Proper manners of bringing up
2.	Nursery	3 to 6 years of age	Play. Fairy tales. Normal recreational activities
3.	Elementary stage	6 to 13 years of age	1. Separate education and curriculum for boys and girls 2. Music, Dance, Poetry 3. Mathematics 4. Religion

Sl. No.	*Stage*	*Age Group*	*Subjects/Activities*
4.	Secondary stage	13 to 16 years of age	1. Religious chorus songs 2. Poem recitation 3. Emphasis on principles of Mathematics 4. Humanities
5.	Gymnastic stage	16 to 20 years of age	Physical education, Military training, No literary education.
6.	Higher education	20 to 30 years of age	1. Algebra 2. Geometry 3. Astronomy 4. Science subjects
7.	Higher Specialised Education	30 to 35 years of age:	Officers training 1. Epistemology 2. Ethics 3. Logic 4. Philosophy 5. Psychology 6. Polity 7. Oratory 8. Law

Plato's Dialectic

The term 'Dialectic' implies Platonic investigation of the eternal ideas, a critical investigation for exposing falsehood and eliciting truth through systematic reasoning. Important subjects included in 'Dialectic' were:

(1) Polity
(2) Philosophy
(3) Ethics
(4) Logic
(5) Psychology

The study of these subjects was aimed at making philosophers and seekers of truth. It developed wisdom to understand complicated matters. These studies lasted for 5 years during the age group 30 to 35 years.

Importance of Mathematics: Next to philosophy, Plato considers mathematics most important. He observed, "Have you further observed that those who have natural talent for calculation are generally quick at every other kind of knowledge?" Similarly he emphasised the importance of geometry. In all departments of knowledge, an experience proves that anyone who has studied geometry is infinitely quicker in apprehension than anyone who has not.

Music Training: Plato is of the view that education should begin during infancy or early years of childhood with music. This is needed to lead a harmonious development of the body as well of the soul. He in this regard said, "Music training is a more potent instrument than any other, because rhythm and harmony find their way into the inward places of the soul, on which they fasten grace".

Physical Training: According to Plato, physical training should come after music training. On the role of physical training, he wrote, "My belief is not that the good boy by any bodily existence improves the soul, but on the contrary that the good soul by her own excellence improves the body as far as this may be possible".

Education of Women: Plato is for the education of women. He does not suggest any separate system of education for women. However, he considers women weaker than men. He writes, "For the patronage of State, men and women are equal but women, are, no doubt, weaker in strength".

Plato's Views on Industrial Education: Plato viewed industrial arts with contempt. According to him carpentry, tailoring, weaving, etc. were the occupations of slaves. These arts could be learnt through family traditions.

Contribution to Educational Thought and Practices

Plato made a deep study of the various aspects of education and keeping in view the socio-econo-politico structure of the society formulated his scheme/plan of education. He adopted idealistic approach in this. He was the first Western educator who paid so much attention to educational issues. He fully accepted the need for planning the system according to the various stages of development of the human being. While evaluating his scheme of education, it must be remembered that since then sea-change has taken place.

Plato's contribution may be summed up as:

1. Plato emphasised the balanced development of the personality.
2. He laid stress on inculcating the values of good citizenship.
3. He advanced moral training.
4. He formulated a definite system of education which included specific curriculum for specific stages.

Limitations of Plato's Views. From the present point of view, following limitations are noticed:

1. He laid too much emphasis on philosophy.
2. He neglected the education of the producing class.
3. He laid more emphasis on mathematics and less on literature.
4. His system of education was based on class system.
5. He paid no attention to the education of the slaves.

4

Aristotle

(384-322 B.C.)

Aristotle, an ancient Greek philosopher is regarded as one of the encyclopaedic writers in the entire range of the European thought. His ideas on ethics and politics are still considered as works studying. He is widely quoted by scholars in their writings. Aristotle was the disciple of Plato. He served as a tutor to Alexander of Macedonia.

Aristotle was the head of the Lyceum (a type of higher education institution). In the field of education, he had made a very valuable contribution.

Aristotle's scheme of education is to be found in the Seventh and Eighth Books (Chapters) of his monumental publication *Politics*. Aristotle considered education as a branch of political science or politics.

Philosophical Thought Regarding Life

According to Aristotle there can be three possible types of life:

1. The lowest type is the sensuous life—life of pleasures and gratification.
2. Higher than this is the life of the warrior and the politician. Aristotle considers this type of life praiseworthy if led among a community of freemen.
3. Aristotle criticises the despotic and tyrannical life which derives pleasure in subjugating people who do not deserve enslavement. He appreciates the political life among equals based on the principle of reciprocity.

Aristotle praised as the highest, the life of the self-sufficient philosophers contemplating eternal truth. "The life of the reason is the highest because reason is the essence of man and is divine in its nature".

Philosophy of Realism and Its Implications

Aristotle never considered man to be completely evil or wicked. He believed that in man there are elements of both self-love and social instinct. In case he is not trained in the art of just, decent and socialised existence then the beastly instincts dominate in him but if he gets training, then he can rise.

Aristotle divides the soul of man into two parts – the irrational and the rational. The irrational part is trained by the cultivation of moral virtues. Moral virtues are acquired by the repetition of the corresponding acts. Although these acts cannot be prescribed exactly, still they must avoid excess and defect. Thus, Aristotle was a great believer in the ethical mean or moderation ('*Madhyam*') way: The mean is difficult to achieve but can be grasped by perception.

A completely happy man is he who acts in accordance with complete virtue and possesses physical prowess, technical competence, mental virtuosity and morality. He advocates the doctrine of golden mean which implies that a virtuous man would be neither super-normal nor sub-normal but justly and wisely normal. Thus his philosophy was of *realism*.

Aristotle follows a middle path in relation to the State and the citizen. His virtue is relative in the sense that the citizen has to act according to the canons of that particular constitution wherein the person is born and resides. But this does not imply, according to Aristotle, that the citizens should perform those actions in which oligarchs and democracies delight but that they should perform those actions by which the existence of an oligarchy or democracy is made possible.

Except for military training other branches of education should receive the maximum degree of autonomy from State interference. This aspect also conforms to *realism*. Aristotle observes that necessary, useful and profitable actions are also essential but they are not ends in themselves.

Aristotle wanted the development of physical strength by gymnastic training but is opposed to mere athleticism acquired by the neglect of other virtues.

According to Aristotle, courage and endurance are needed for business and action, philosophy or wisdom for leisure, and temperance and justice are needed for both action and leisure.

FEATURES OF EDUCATIONAL PHILOSOPHY AND PRACTICES

Meaning and Aim of Education

According to Aristotle, education is the process of systematic training and instruction whereby the citizen may be enabled to realise the synthesis of the ideals of the best man and the best citizen. Aristotle states that the goods of the mind cannot be attained without an adequate supply of goods of the body. Thus education implies 'creation of a sound mind in a sound body'.

Education, according to Aristotle is the art of acquiring happiness and not the pursuit of pleasure.

Aristotle, however, lays more emphasis on making an individual a good human being. "In the virtue of each, the virtue of all is involved". In his book *Politics* Aristotle dealt with the individual rather than social aspect of education.

Three Stages in the Development of an Individual

Aristotle points out the following three stages in the development of the individual:

1. The period of physical growth.
2. The period of irrational appetites or passions.
3. The period of reason.

Curriculum

Aristotle prescribed the following curriculum:

(a) *Gymnastic and Drill* for the development of the body not to make brainless athlete but to ensure a sound bodily condition. He wrote in *Politics*: "It is grace and not brute strength that should count for most, for it is not the wolf or any of the lower animals that can engage in any fine and dangerous contest, but the good man".

(b) *Inculcation of good habits* without which the irrational soul of the child may be led astray by pleasures from wrong things. This implies training of character.

(c) *Music* for supplying occupation for leisure. According to Aristotle, "Music is able to modify the character of the soul".

(d) *Study of biology and natural history* followed by a study of metaphysics for the intellectual education of the young.

(e) *Art and literature, science and religion* for teaching the man business of war and peace, the useful and the fine.

Curriculum for Different Stages/Ages

1. First Seven Years: Stress on physical education.
2. Seven to Fourteen years: Reading and writing. Music etc.
3. Fourteen to Twenty One Years: Arithmetic, Biology and Geometry, Metaphysics, etc.
4. After Twenty Years of Age: Politics, Religion and Psychology for administrative work, war and peace.

Habit Formation

Aristotle attaches great importance to habits in the realisation of the moral nature of man and accordingly gives it a fundamental place in education. Habit is defined by him in his book *Metaphysics*: "Having a habit means a disposition to that which is either well disposed or ill disposed, and either in itself or with reference to something else, e.g., health is a habit, for it is such a disposition. We speak of a habit if there is a portion of such a disposition, and even the excellence of the parts is a habit of the whole thing".

Training in habit formation must come earlier than rational training. From the very early years Aristotle wants the children to be habituated to hard life.

Moral Education

The main categories of moral virtues are courage, friendliness, justice, liberality, magnificence, magnani-mity, temperance, and truthfulness. Aristotle had liked to include ready wit as a moral virtue. He calls upon the educators to control the use and circulation of stories etc. in order that from the very childhood the future citizens may learn temperance. Temperance is a cardinal virtue in Aristotle's book *Ethics*. Aristotle states that moral training is not complete in itself. It is for the growth of intellectual enlightenment.

Significance of the Teaching-Learning of Music: Aristotle lists the following merits of music:

1. Music is a source of harmless pleasure.
2. Music provides recreation.
3. Music has a purgative influence – *Katharsis*.
4. Music is needed for forming character because it habituates the mind to the love of that which is good and noble.
5. Music provides intellectual enjoyment in leisure.

Aristotle is opposed to professional competence in music. He only wants an amateurish understanding of music. He is against passion-exciting music.

Evaluation of Aristotle's Views

Aristotle was a realist; he observed what education is and emphasised that the way children ought to be instructed should be very clear to the instructors/teachers. Education would differ according to the nature of the State.

Aristotle's views on the teaching and training of moral virtues are quite relevant even today. He is fully justified in stressing 'habituation' for the practice of moral virtues.

Aristotle is mindful of the synthesis of knowledge and happiness.

Aristotle was a *realist* and his *realism* is manifest in his approach to life and educational ideas and practices. He fully took note of the prevailing scenario and accordingly formulated his scheme of education.

5

Erasmus Desiderius
(1467-1536)

A Dutch educator and humanist, Erasmus is popularly known for his masterpiece *Praise of Folly.* He is also known as 'Prince of Humanism'. Thomas More, the author of *Utopia,* who was Lord Chancellor of England, was his best friend.

He was ordained as a priest in 1492. After 1495, he lived an independent life, gave lessons to the sons of rich bourgeois and aristocratic English and German families.

Erasmus wrote textbooks which later became teaching manuals and remained in use for centuries in schools such as St. Paul's School and Eton College in England.

Erasmus established a reputation as an 'orator and poet' in humanist circles. He taught for many years at Cambridge University before finally settling down in Switzerland. Erasmus ridiculed religious superstitions but did not support the more direct attacks of men like Martin Luther on the Church.

Publications on Education

1. *On the Right Method of Instruction.*
2. *On the Liberal Education of Boys from the Beginning.*
3. *Education of the Christian Man.*
4. *The Education of the Christian Prince.*
5. *On a Liberal Education for Children.*
6. *Literacy and Educational Writings.* (Ed. J. Kelley Swards).

Erasmus wrote several works for his own pupils, including:

- *The Twofold Abundance of Words and Things*—dealing with rhetoric, grammar and syntax, style and Latin elegance.
- *On Letter Writing*—an absorbing manual or the art of writing.
- *On the Correct Pronunciation of Latin and Greek.*
- *Comparisons and Similarities.*

- *On the Civility of Children's Behaviour*—Children should be given a liberal education from a very early age.

Philosophy of Education

Erasmus's philosophy has two noteworthy characteristics: The individual implications of education and the social implications of education.

He pointed out three elements which were important.

(a) Nature (innate capacity of the individual),
(b) Training - skilled application of instruction and guidance,
(c) Free exercise of the activity and behaviour implanted by nature and training.

About the social implications of education, Erasmus observed that education is a matter as much of social concern as of individual concern.

Erasmus laid importance of beginning a child's education from the earliest years. He pointed out that the parents and the state are obliged to educate a child in the interest of the State. He wrote: "It is a public obligation in no way inferior to the ordering of the army".

Educational Ideals

Erasmus turned to the past for the ideals of social regeneration. He looked to the secular institutions of ancient Greece and Rome. Erasmus was satisfied with the establishment of a small aristocracy of intellect.

Education of Children at Home

Erasmus preferred education at home under the guidance of a tutor carefully chosen by the parents.

Liberal Education

Jean Claude Margolin explains the concept of liberal education as interpreted by Erasmus in these words,

> "For Erasmus, to educate young people was to educate adults, inasmuch as—and this he deeply believed—the future of individuals and the quality of their lives depended, in large measure, on the education they had received in their youth. "A man is not born a man, but becomes one" is the vigorous assertion of one of the sayings in the *De pueris*

whereby Erasmus distinguishes man from all other creatures—"A dog remains a dog and an oak an oak, because they are no more than that with which nature has endowed them, once and for always. But human beings, thanks to the reason with which God endowed them when He created them, can improve their primitive nature; education will achieve this on condition that it is 'liberal', which means based on free will (which even children possess), and that the tutor has the wisdom and skill to use persuasion and gentleness, rather than brutally imposing precepts and dogmas".

Emphasis on Classical Literature

Erasmus took no interest in the vernacular literature. His sources of deriving the substance of knowledge were the Greek and Latin languages. His conviction was that the classical works contained all essential knowledge.

Place of Grammar

Regarding the place of grammar in the teaching of literature Erasmus said:

> "It is not by learning rules that we acquire the power of speaking a language but by daily intercourse with those accustomed to express themselves with exactness and refinement and by the copious reading of the best authors".

He insisted that grammar should be kept strictly subordinate to the content. He considered formal grammar necessary but stated that it should be preceded by an informal acquaintance with the language through conversation on all kinds of subjects and on all facets of life.

Teaching and Learning Methods

The methods advocated by Erasmus are surprisingly modern in their historical context. The methods are a complete departure with the scholastic methods of Middle Ages which were based on learning by rote. Competition was encouraged among children. There was no place for the traditional corporal punishment.

Women's Education

Erasmus shared the views of all his contemporaries that girls had no need of advanced intellectual education since their lot was either to marry, have children and keep house or to enter a convent.

To sum up, the works of Erasmus are so wide-ranging and varied in both content and form that he is sometimes called the 'Tutor of Europe'. His contribution has been summed up by Margolin as—

> "A teacher and educational adviser to the schoolmasters of his time, Erasmus became, by vocation and also because circumstances required it of him, the theoretician at one and the same time of a political philosophy based on peace and the protection of the people by their prince, of a code of religious ethics concerning the status of women, and of a renovated theology based on scrupulous interpretation of the Gospels and on rhetoric, which is used by the preacher in the exercise of his function".

In Erasmus, the humanist outweighed the reformer.

6

Michel De Montaigne (1533-92)

Montaigne was a French essayist, moralist and educational theorist. His *Essays* are particularly a good illustration of the 'cultural mosaic' of Renaissance. His views on education are found scattered through many of his *Essays*, but particularly in *Concerning the Education of Children*.

Montaigne believed in the 'training of judgement' than mere book learning, because "To know by heart is not to know at all; it is merely to retain what one has entrusted to his memory".

Montaigne further stated, "I would rather prefer wisdom-judgement, civil customs and modest behaviour than base and literal learning".

Montaigne's Negative Education

Prof. Gerard Wormser explains Montaigne's negative education in an article in *Prospects*, 84(1/2), Vol. 3, 1994 as: "Montaigne calls for a more radical interpretation. Learning provides no positive standard; it merely enables us to know how far the conduct of individuals departs from what a wise nature would prompt. Besides being incorrigible, faculties are distributed at random. Education serves above all to bring them out so that the best characters can be discovered. This is what Montaigne has in mind when he jestingly recommends that the tutor should quickly strangle the unworthy pupil when nobody is looking or apprentice him to some trade which will keep him occupied. Education would thus mainly serve a negative purpose, seeking to cast our vices likely to develop and become a danger to human society.

"Unconvinced of the influence education was supposed to have on us, Montaigne has no difficulty in showing how the natural disposition comes out under all circumstances or sets impassable limits to everyone's behaviour, even if that natural disposition is concealed by disguises and masks which give it false colours and belie it".

Need for Efficient Tutors from the Early Stages for Forming Moral Behaviour

The same writer explains Montaigne's views in these words: "Habit, even when based on a figment of the imagination 'gradually and stealthily... slides her authoritative foot into us; then, having by this gentle and humble beginning planted it firmly within us, helped by time she later discloses an angry tyrannous countenance, against which we are no longer allowed even to lift up our eyes'. Whereupon Montaigne concludes that 'our greatest vices do acquire their bent during our most tender infancy, so that our formation is chiefly in the hands of our wet-nurses'. The hold which imagination and habit acquire over children's attitudes can therefore be judged from their earliest expression. If children are not taught to detest their natural vices, 'whatever mask they hide behind', 'what is the use of educating them?' Whatever our opinion on the matter, we must realise that all behaviour, all value judgements, are based to some extent on habit, or custom, for the habits, or customs, of the place where you were born, widely though these may differ from one place to another, rule your conscience. This line of thought is continued in the brief essay on credulity, 'That it is madness to judge the true and the false from our own capacities': 'How many of the things which constantly come into our purview must be deemed monstrous or miraculous if we apply such terms to anything which outstrips our reason!'

"The essence of any education is thus the way in which it inculcates moral principles consistent with the goal of wisdom and calculated to develop a conscience enabling us all to bring our behaviour in line with incontestable standards. For this reason, Montaigne mercilessly mocks teachers who, unable to get the children to assimilate what they are taught, are content with puffing them up with it, making them conceited and arrogant: Learned we may be with another man's learning: we can only be wise with wisdom of our own'. Hence, since I would prefer that he turned out to be an able man nor an erudite one, I would wish you to be careful to select as guide for him a tutor with a well-formed rather than a well-filled brain'.

"Only on this condition can we rediscover the Socratic method of teaching by means of exercises in which the pupil shows his capacity for discernment".

Teaching by Dialogue

Montaigne advocates teaching by dialogue. He wrote, "To follow another is to follow nothing"... "the boy will transform his borrowings; he will confound their forms so that the end-product is entirely his: namely, his judgement, the forming of which is the only aim of his toil, his study and his education. Let him hide the help he received and put only his achievements on display".

7

Jan Amos Comenius (1592-1670)

Jan Amos Komensky, born on March 28, 1592 in Moravia, now part of the Czech Republic, is generally known as Comenius—Latinised form of his name (Jean Piaget in *Prospects*, Vol. X & III, No. 1-12, 1993). Comenius was of a piercing nature from his early childhood. He did not like the prevailing system of education. He had an open mind and did not hesitate to receive education from any kind and from any place. He travelled extensively and established contact with the scholars of his time through correspondence.

He was educated at Heidelberg University in Germany. Subsequently, he became a clergyman. Upon his return to his native place, he served as a school teacher and later as the Church Pastor at Fulnek. The start of the Thirty Years' War was the beginning of his misfortunes and he was forced to flee his homeland. In 1628 Comenius settled in Leszno, Poland, where he wrote his books calling for the reform of the educational system. His publications earned him reputation in other countries and he was invited first to England, and then to Sweden and Hungary to reform school systems.

Major Publications

1. *The Great Didactic*
2. *The School of Infancy*
3. *The Gate to Languages Unlocked*
4. *Visible World in Pictures*

Views on Various Dimensions of Education

Concept of Education: Comenius believed that education is not limited to the action of the school and family but is a part of general social life.

Nature of the Child and the Role of the Teacher: Comenius was of the firm view that the teachers should understand how a child's mind develops and learns.

Books for Children: Comenius was the first to use an illustrated book for children — *Visible World in Pictures* (1658).

Teaching Techniques: Comenius is best known for his contribution to teaching techniques. He tends to mention the following principles to reform techniques of teaching:

1. Whatever is taught, its objective should be made clear.
2. Learning material should have practical utility.
3. General rules should be explained before hand.
4. All topics should be taught in a sequential manner.
5. The matter should not be left unless the child understands it clearly.
6. All topics as far as possible should be taught in a correlated manner.
7. Thinking on the part of the child should be encouraged.
8. Whatever is to be taught to the child should be taught in direct and in clear words.
9. Education should not be made a complex affair.

Discipline as a Great Motive Power

Comenius explains the importance of discipline in the life of a school in *The Great Didactic*: "There is a proverb in Bohemia, 'A school without discipline is like a mill without water', and this is very true. For example, if you withdraw the water from a mill, it stops and in the same way, if you deprive a school of discipline, you take away from it its motive power. A field also, if it is never ploughed, produces nothing but weeds, and trees if not continually pruned, revert to their wild state and bear no fruit. It must not be thought, however, that we wish our schools to resound with shrieks and blows. What we demand is vigilance and attention on the part of the master and of the pupils for discipline is nothing but an unfailing method by which we may make our scholars in reality".

Discipline to be Always Watchful

He goes to explain the concept of discipline as, "Our enemy, Satan, is on the watch not only while we are asleep but also while we are awake and as we sow good seeds in the minds of our pupils, he continues to plant his own weeds there as well and sometimes a corrupt nature brings forth weeds of its own accord, so that these evil dispositions must be kept in check by force. We must, therefore, strike against them by means of discipline, that is to say, using blame and punishment which should always be administered on the spot, that the vice may be checked as soon as it shows itself, or may be, as far as possible, torn up by the roots. Discipline, therefore, should be ever watchful, not with the view of enforcing application to study (for learning is always attractive to the minds, if it be treated with the right method) but to ensure clearly morals".

'Why', 'When' and 'How' of Discipline

Comenius considers punishment "like a bitter draught presented for them (for children) by the doctor". He explains the 'Why', 'When' and 'When' of punishment as "Punishment should be employed towards those who err. But it is not because they have erred that they should be punished (for what has been done cannot be undone), but in order that they may not err again in the future. Discipline, therefore, should be free from personal elements, such as anger or dislike and should be exercised with such frankness and sincerity of purpose, that even the pupils may feel that the action taken is for their good, and that those sit over them are but exercising paternal authority. They will thus regard it in the same light as a bitter draught prescribed for them by the doctor".

Setting a Work on Scientific Principle

Comenius advised to learn a lesson from nature. "The very sun in the heaven gives us a lesson on this point. In early spring, when plants are young and tender, it does not scorch them but warms and invigorates with slow degrees not putting forth its full heat until they are full-grown and bring forth fruit and seeds. The gardener proceeds on the same principle, and does not apply the pruning-knife to plants that are immature. In the same way, a musician does not strike his lyre a blow with his fist or with a stick, nor does he throw it against the wall because it produces discordant sound, but setting a work on scientific principle, he tunes it and gets it into order".

Contribution

Addressing the winners of the Comenius Medal, in 1988, in Paris, then Director-General of UNESCO, Mr. Federico Mayor said that 'among the eminent educators of the past, Comenius is one of those who incarnates in the best possible way the image one may have of a UNESCO precursor. His philosophy that encouraged political unity, religious reconciliation and international cooperation in the field of education... has lost nothing of its actuality'.

In the words of Jean Piaget, "Comenius was the first to conceive the full-scale science of education". His educational objective can be summed up in the axiom on the title page of *The Great Didactic*, 'Teaching Thoroughly All Things To All Men'. He is also considered to be the first educator to have put forward the concept of international education. His ideas on education for everyone and for all peoples, and on the international organisation of public education make him a fore-runner of many modern institutions and trends of thought. Comenius' efforts on behalf of universal education earned him the title of 'Teacher of Nations'.

(*Source*: '*Educational Innovation*' No. 98. March 1999, IBE-Geneva)

8

Jean Jacques Rousseau
(1712-1778)

Rousseau was a Swiss educational reformer and thinker. He had the flash of a genius that seemed to attract followers and friends despite his self confessed bad habits and shortcomings. His writings have exercised such an influence on educational theory and practice that they are widely quoted even today. There is no doubt that he is considered one of the great leaders of the world.

Early Childhood

Rousseau lost his mother at an early age. His father was a poor watch-maker and could not provide him regular schooling. Rousseau left school at the age of 12. He tried unsuccessfully all sorts of occupations—apprentice to a rotary and then to an engraver etc. He became a music critic for sometime at Paris. From the age of twelve to twenty nine years, he remained a vagabond and during his wanderings he met different types of people, learnt to sympathise with the poor. He developed love for nature. He also defied the conventional rules of society.

Interest in Education

His experiences at different places awoke in him a keen interest in the problem of education. At about the age of about 25, he studied Hobbes, Locke, Montaigne, Pascal, Voltaire Malebranche, Leibnitz and Desccartes.

Rousseau's Suicide

Rousseau revolted against the established (canons) of society and advocated the doctrine of "Back to nature". He wrote, "Man is born free and every where he is in chains". His ideas were vehemently opposed by the establishment. His books were burnt. He incurred the displeasure of the French authorities and had to live in exile for many years. He was so much disgusted and disappointed that he committed suicide in 1778. However, his greatness was recognised later and his views had tremendous influence on the outbreak of the French Revolution in 1789.

Publications and Essence of His Writings

After wandering for a number of years, he settled down in Paris (France). In 1750, at the age of 38, Rousseau wrote his first book *The Progress of the Art and the Science*. This was followed by *The Origin of Inequality Among Men* (1753), *The New Heloise – a romance* (1759); *Social Contract* (1762), and *Emile* or *Concerning Education* (1762).

In his publications, he criticised the existing institutions. He attributed the existing oppression and corruption of the society to the advancement of civilisation, which according to him was the main cause of the differences and inequalities among men. Regarding the absolute powers of the sovereign, Rousseau wrote, "He cannot impose upon his subjects fetters that are useless to the community".

Educational Philosophy

'Return to nature' was the theme of his two educational publications (novels): *The New Heloise* (1761) and *Emile* (1762). These books, were among the most widely read of the popular writing of the century.

Rousseau was an arch enemy of child neglect. His *Emile* made Europe child conscious. It is still widely quoted in almost all books on educational philosophy, principles and practices.

Sources of Education

According to Rousseau following are the three main sources of education:

1. *Education of Nature*: "The constitutional exertion of our organs and faculties is the education of nature".
2. *Education given by Men*: "The uses we are taught to make of that exertion, constitute the education given to us by men".
3. *Education from Circumstances*: "And in the acquisition made by our own experience, on the objects that surround us, consists our education from circumstances".

By education from nature he meant development according to the child's endowments and capacities. By education from men, he emphasised the importance of social environment, teaching how to make use of that development. By education from things, he understood physical environment, helping to gain experience by ourselves. He says that harmonious development of these three factors constitutes an ideal scheme of education.

Such harmony in education is possible by subordinating the education of men and things to that of nature because we have no control over nature. We, must, therefore, direct the other two, to ensure cooperation of these factors for imparting ideal education.

Theory of Negative Education

Rousseau believed that everything is good as it comes from nature and it generates in the hands of man, so he advocated that the education of the child should be purely negative. The child should not be taught the principles of truth and virtue but guarded against evil. He wrote, "I call a positive education one that tends to form the mind prematurely and to instruct the child in the duties that belong to him. I call negative education one that tends to perfect the organs that are the instruments of knowledge and endeavours to process the way for reasons, by the proper exercises of senses".

Aims of Education

Rousseau's aim of education was the attainment of fullest natural growth of the individual, leading to balanced, harmonious useful and natural life. The real aim of education is to help the child to live his life. He says, "To live is not merely to breathe. It is to act, to make use of our organs, senses, our faculties and of all those parts of ourselves, which give us the feeling of our existence".

This general aim of education was split up by Rousseau according to the nature at different stages of human development.

(i) *Infancy, i.e.,* from birth to the age of five years, the aim of education is to develop a well-regulated freedom.

(ii) *In childhood, i.e.,* between the age of five and twelve, the main aim of education is to provide the child with the strength which he needs for the attainment of well-regulated freedom.

(iii) *In boyhood or pre-adolescent period, i.e.,* from twelve years to fifteen years the aim of education is "to acquire such knowledge which may satisfy the wants of the child and must be functionally useful". This is the period for intellectual education—the period of instruction, labour and study.

(iv) *In adolescent period, i.e.,* from 15 to 20 years, the aim of education is the training of heart, to make the child loving and tender-hearted so that he may live peacefully in social relationship. In this period, religious, moral and social education is recommended. In the previous periods, the child has already developed physically and intellectually. He must now grow emotionally, aesthetically, socially and morally. The sex instinct, which is sufficiently developed by this time, is to be sublimated by re-directing it to the love of some noble idea and by keeping the young occupied in work and activity.

Curriculum

Rousseau recommends curriculum in accordance with the nature of each stage of the child.

Curriculum at the First Stage: Curriculum at the first stage (from one to 5 years) would be such as it develops physical strength. The child should be allowed to wander freely in the countryside. His play-things should be very simple such as branches with fruits and flowers and no expensive toys. 'Let him not be pampered! Let him not be subdued'.

Curriculum at the Second Stage: Curriculum at the second stage (between 5 to 12 years) should lead to the development of senses. Rousseau thinks that if senses are not trained properly, independent reasoning and judgement are impossible. Emile (the hero of the novel *Emile)* is to be given the greatest freedom of physical movement, simple diet and light clothing. There will be no verbal lessons for him. He will not be instructed in language, history and geography. Emile is to learn from his own experience. No moral instruction is to be given. "Exercise the body, the organs, the senses and powers but keep the soul lying fallow as long as you can. Training for senses means learning to judge, foresee and reason through them. It is more than the mere use of them. All learning must come by play-way. There is no need for the child to learn anything by heart. For Emile there is no curriculum. He has to learn by activity and experience.

Curriculum at the Third Stage: Curriculum at the third stage of pre-adolescence (12 to 15 years) should be built around curiosity which should create an urge for knowledge. Rousseau states that this is the period for developing intellect. Emile is introduced to studies that reveal nature, astronomy, science and the arts and crafts. Rousseau emphasises the learning of manual and industrial arts partly to make Emile independent and partly to overcome the prejudice held against the manual work. Rousseau wanted that the boy must be taken from one workshop to another and he must try his hand at every trade. In this way Rousseau wanted to teach him industrial exchange, banking and transportation. Rousseau does not recommend the study of books. The only book he recommends is *Robinson Crusoe*, a study of life according to nature.

Curriculum at the Fourth Stage: In the fourth stage of the adolescence period (15 to 20 years of age), training of heart should receive attention. In the earlier stages, the boy was an individual working for self-perfection and self-development. Now he has to be social and adapt himself to the conduct and interest of others. The study of society, politics, economics, history and religion are the appropriate studies for the youth to understand complex social relationships. Emile must be provided opportunities for training in moral education about his relations with his fellow men and moral qualities such as benevolence, kindness, service and sympathy. Rousseau recommends that moral education should be given through activities and occupations and not through lectures on ethics. History will be utilised as a means of moral instruction. Travel is recommended for knowing the world and the institutions of the neighbouring countries. At this stage the youth undergoes a new birth on account of the appearance of sex impulse. Sex instruction is to consist of direct moral exhortation on chastity and an explanation of the mysteries of creation in the world of plants, animals and men in a dispassionate manner.

Education of Women: Rousseau maintained that women were the makers of men. They were, "the chaste guardians of our morals, and the sweet security of our place". Their education was to be different from men. Rousseau believed that "Woman is made specially to please man". She has, therefore, to be taught to be soft and sweet and learn to suffer and bear the wrongs of her husband without complaint". The duty of women towards man is "to train him in childhood, to tend him in manhood, and to counsel him throughout his life". Rousseau, therefore, advocated that her studies, should be practical. Intellectual interests, he believed, destroyed her nature. He stated, "I would a hundred times prefer a simple girl, rudely brought up to a girl of learning".

He remarked, "A woman of literacy education (culture) is the plague of her husband; her children, her family her servants—everybody". Sophie, therefore, is to learn embroidery, lace making, the art of house decorating and house keeping, sewing etc.

Methods of Teaching

Observation of the Nature of the Child: Rousseau wrote, "I wish some discreet person would give us a treatise on the art of observing children—an art which would be of immense value to us but of which parents and schoolmasters have not yet learnt the very first rudiment".

Art of Teaching: Rousseau further said, "To know how to suggest is the art of teaching".

Rousseau emphasised, "The highest function of the teacher consists not much in imparting knowledge as in stimulating the pupil in its love and pursuit".

He was against the harsh and unsympathetic methods of education which repressed the natural inclinations and tendencies of the child. He advocated simple and direct methods of instruction and urged "experience before expression" and "objects before words". He said, "Give your scholar no verbal lesson. He should be taught by experience alone. Teach by doing whenever you can and only fall back upon words when doing is out of question. Book knowledge should be as little as possible". Emphasising "object teaching", he remarked, "let the senses always be the guides. Let there be no books but the world and no other instruction than facts. The child who reads, does not think, he merely reads. He is not receiving instruction but learning words".

Methods of teaching advocated by Rousseau are summed up as under:

1. Do not teach books. "I hate books. They only teach us to talk about things that we know nothing about. To conceal

their deficiencies teachers choose the dead languages—words, words, words".

2. Provide opportunities to children from their own experience and not from books.

   "Let him (the child) not be taught science, let him discover it".

3. Provide sense training.
4. Never substitute the symbol a thing unless it is impossible to show the thing itself.

Role of the Teacher

Rousseau assigns a minor place to the teacher in the educative process. He is not called an instructor but only a guide. His main responsibility is to motivate the child to learn. This he can achieve by exploiting the innate tendencies of the child. He must possess a profound understanding of the child's nature and be able to control his emotional reactions. He is not to impose any rules of control upon the child. He is to allow him perfect freedom and guide him properly.

Rousseau wrote, "The highest function of the teacher consists not so much in imparting knowledge as on stimulating the pupil in its love and pursuit". Further he advises, "To know how to suggest is the art of teaching". Rousseau placed stress on developing the reasoning power of the child. He observed, "If ever you (teacher) substitute authority in the place of argument, he (child) will reason no longer, he will ever afterwards be handed like a shuttle cork between the opinion of others".

Freedom of the Child—Discipline by Natural Consequences

He believes in freedom of the child. It is only in a free atmosphere that the child will be able to develop his inborn and innate capacities. He does not believe in punishing the child so as to correct his future behaviour. The reason behind this assumption according to Rousseau is very simple-the child is not able to link up the punishment administered and the mischief done by him. Children, therefore, should be left alone to experience the consequences of the mischief done by them. Nature, according to Rousseau, is a great teacher. If children commit mistakes and violate the principles of nature, they naturally invite the retribution of nature. This conception in the field of education is known as "Discipline by natural consequences".

Secondly, in the field of education, Rousseau starts with the assumption that the nature of child is essentially good, hence he should have freedom in his actions. Firstly, he believes that the child will not commit any immoral act, and secondly, even if he commits any, he will learn morality by the natural consequences of the action done.

His concept of freedom and discipline is summed up as:

1. Discipline by natural consequences.
2. No punishments.
3. Full freedom to the child.

'*Emile*': An Important Treatise on Education

'*Emile*' is a treatise on education cast in the form of a novel in which there are three characters; Emile, who may be regarded as 'Rousseau' while a boy, and his tutor, who is obviously Rousseau, as a man, Sophie, who is destined to be the mate of Emile.

'*Emile*' consists of five books or parts on training and education.

Book I deals with the infant; Book II with childhood; Book III with the pre–adolescent between the ages of twelve and fifteen; Book IV with adolescence; and Book V with the education of girls.

Lord Morley has described the value of '*Emile*' in these words:

> "It touched the deeper things of character. It filled parents with a sense of the dignity of their task. It cleared away the accumulation of clogging prejudices and obscure inveterate usage, which made education one of the dark formalistic arts. It admitted floods of light and air into the tightly closed nurseries and school rooms. It effected the substitution of growth for mechanism... It was the charter of youthful deliverance".

On the other hand, the Parliament of Paris criticised '*Emile*' and ordered to be burnt publicly. Orders for the arrest of Rousseau were issued and he had to run away from France to Switzerland. The reading of *Emile* was forbidden by the Archbishop of Paris. The book was condemned on account of 'Containing an abominable doctrine, ready to subvert natural law and to destroy the foundations of the Christian religion...

tending to trouble the peace of States, to cause subjects to revolt against their sovereigns; as containing a large number of prepositions false, scandalous, full of hate against the Church, derogatory to the respect of holy scriptures .... erroneous, impious, blasphemous and heretical".

Rousseau's Naturalism and His Theory of Negative Education

The term negative education denotes Rousseau's hatred for the formal educational system prevailing in the society. He considered it unnatural and against the nature of child. He vehemently criticised it and advocated to replace it. Since the formal system was considered as the positive system of education, he termed his own system of education as negative. It will be seen from the following characteristics of the negative education, that they are at variance with that of the positive system of education.

Characteristics of Negative Education

The following are the chief characteristics of his theory of Negative Education:

1. *Direct Experience of the Child*: Rousseau would like Emile to learn from his own experiences and not from books. Knowledge acquired from books is second-hand and easily forgotten. Personal knowledge directly acquired, from various learning situations, is something permanent, which the child will not forget. This will constitute the permanent nature of his character.

2. *The Heuristic Method*: Rousseau also advocates the heuristic method of teaching. He would like to place the child in the position of an original discoverer. The child will learn science with self-made and self-invented apparatus. The same method is to be applied to other subjects of the curriculum.

3. *No Time Saving in Childhood*: According to Rousseau, in childhood no time should be saved. It should rather be lost. Let the child run, jump and play all day long. In all these activities he will have a continuous reconstruction of experience which is nothing but education, pure and simple. Time lost on play and recreational activities in childhood, is not lost but profitably gained; childhood is not the time for intellectual pursuits.

4. *No Book Learning:* Rousseau says, "I hate books because they are a curse to children. They teach us to talk only that which we do not know. Instead of making the child stick to his books, I keep

him busy in the workshop; his hands will work to the profit of his mind".

5. *No Habit Formation*: In his own words, "The only habit which the child should be allowed to form is to contract no habit at all". Young children should not be made slaves of rigid habits. They should be left free in all their activities. If any habits are to be formed in childhood, let them form natural habits.

6. *No Direct Moral Education*: Rousseau is not in favour of teaching of morals. Let the child be left free to act and learn what is right and wrong, by the consequences of his own actions. He says, "Much more harm than good is done by your ceaseless preaching and moralising". He further says, "Inflict on the child no sort of punishment and never make him ask your pardon. As there is no moral quality in his actions, he can do nothing wrong".

7. *No Formal Discipline: Discipline by Natural Consequences.* Rousseau is in favour of free and positive discipline for children. Let the children suffer natural consequences of their own actions without the intervention of human beings to protect or punish and in this way they will set themselves right. If a child breaks a window pane, let him sit in the cold wind that gushes in as a result of his folly. If he climbs a tree, let him fall down and learn not to do so again.

8. *No Sticking to Traditional Procedure of Education*: Rousseau was greatly disgusted with the prevailing social, political, economic, religious and educational conditions in his country. So he said, "Follow the reverse of the current practice and you will almost do right". He challenged the traditional procedure of education saying, "Give me a child of twelve who knows nothing at all. At fifteen I will restore him to you, knowing as much as those who have been under instruction from infancy, with the difference that your scholar only knows things by heart, while mine knows how to use his knowledge".

9. *Individual Instruction*: Rousseau emphasised the due importance of individual instruction. He believed that the individuality of the child should be recognised by the educator and duly respected by him. He was right when he said that children are children before they become men.

10. *The Principle of Learning by Doing*: He lays stress on the principle of learning by doing. He says, teach by doing whenever

you can and only fall back on words when doing is out of question. He believes that the child should take part in various activities and learn in a natural way. When the child wants to do something with his own hands his urge to creative activity must be satisfied.

11. *Example is Better than Precept*: For imparting moral education Rousseau believes in the principle that example is better than precept. There is no use lecturing on morality to him; he should have an example of moral behaviour and opportunities may be provided to him to practise virtue.

12. *Social Knowledge by Social Participation*: The child in his period of adolescence will get knowledge about social relations by actually visiting places and coming in contact with the members of the community.

Limitations of Naturalism in Education

1. Physical nature alone is not sufficient for providing education.
2. Naturalism in its extreme form neglects books and other media.
3. Naturalism ignores the higher ends in the education process.
4. It is very difficult to find naturalistic surroundings for locating educational institutions.
5. Naturalism assigns very little importance to teacher in the educative process.
6. Absolute freedom to child is a myth. It cannot exist. Child cannot be allowed the freedom to hang himself.
7. Naturalism does not offer definite aims of education.
8. Rousseau never tried to put into practice his theory and principles of education. Rousseau's naturalism seems to be a utopian concept.
9. Rousseau's views on women education are not in accordance with their nature. Rather they are outmoded in the present context.

Contribution to Education

Notwithstanding some limitations of Rousseau's views in the present context, his contribution to educational theory and principles is very valuable. He ushered in a new era for child education. His major contribution are as under:

1. Rousseau propounded the new gospel of faith in the nature of the child in place of the old ones.
2. His emphasis on the 'discovery' and 'recognition' of childhood traits has brought about a revolutionary change in the thinking of educators.
3. His stress on the 'concrete' led to 'Learning by Doing'.
4. Rousseau anticipated the modern heuristic Method when he declared the child as a 'discoverer'.
5. Rousseau showed the way to the teacher that he must study the child thoroughly.
6. It is due to Rousseau that the need for sense training and physical activities in the earlier development of the child has been recognised in the modern system of education.
7. His concepts of freedom, growth, interest and activity are noteworthy in educational theory and practice.
8. Rousseau showed the value of motivation and of creating problems and of utilising the senses and activities of the child.
9. Present day emphasis on vocational education finds its root in Rousseau.
10. The concept of discipline in naturalism is very desirable. Punishment is based on the consequences of wrong deeds. Children share freedom as well as responsibility.
11. Naturalism in education draws our attention to the aesthetic aspect of surroundings. This also implies that schools should be located in natural surroundings. Education can be imparted in the open.

Robert Rusk describes the work of Rousseau in these words, "Rousseau nevertheless stands to modern education as Plato to ancient education".

According to Charles W. Coulter and Richard S. Rimanoczy, the impact of Rousseau may be stated as "Rousseau made Europe more child-conscious and the formal European educational system more self-conscious'.

P.P. Graves observes in *A Student's History of Education*: "Disregarding the weak and offensive personality of the author, and forgetting the inconsistencies and the contradictions of the work itself, the '*Emile*' has always been accounted a work of great richness, power and underlying wisdom, and each of its defects is more than balanced by a corresponding merit".

Essence of Rousseau's Naturalism

Rousseau is the most prominent naturalist. As a matter of fact Rousseau and naturalism are inseparable. We cannot think of naturalism without Rousseau.

The key-note of Rousseau's philosophy is to have a 'State of Nature', 'Natural Man' and 'Natural Civilisation'.

'Return to nature' was his slogan. He observed, "Everything is good as it comes from the hands of nature but everything degenerates in the hands of man". Again he wrote, "Civilised man is born, lives and dies in the state of slavery. Leave him alone".

According to Rousseau, the state of nature in which man lived long ago was a blissful state. Modern civilisation is the main cause of the misery of mankind. The alternative before mankind is back to nature. The customary procedures of the civilised society should be done away with and the natural state may be accepted again.

Regarding the state of children in the prevailing state of affairs of society, Rousseau wrote, "The age of cheerfulness and gaiety is spent in the midst of tears, punishments, threats and slavery. We torment the poor creatures, for their future good: and perceive not that death is at hand, and ready to seize them amidst all this sorrowful preparation for life. Who can tell how many children have fallen victims to the extravagant sagacity of their parents and guardians? Happy to escape such cruelty, the only advantage the poor suffers reaped from the evils they endured, being to die without regretting a life of misery.

"Man, be humane! It is the first, the chief of moral duties, to exercise humanity to everything, of whatever age or condition, that is relative to man. What! Is wisdom void of humanity? Have a tender regard for children".

Rousseau contends that all the ills and miseries of civilisation are on account of a departure from a 'State of Nature'.

9

Immanuel Kant

(1724-1804)

Kant was an idealist philosopher. He belonged to the family of Pietists, a sect of German Puritans. He studied physics, astronomy, logic and psychology. He dipped into the abstractions of metaphysics, and the realities of algebra, geometry and physics at the University of Konigsberg.

Publications

1. *The Critique of Pure Reason.*
2. *The Critique of Practical Reason.*
3. *The Critique of Judgment.*
4. *On Physical Education.*
5. *On Practical Education.*

The Critique of Pure Reason: Kant maintains that our knowledge does not entirely come through our senses which are but imperfect measures of reality. The real world is beyond our sensory comprehension but not beyond our intellectual comprehension. He said, "The eye without the mind is blind and impotent".

The Critique of Practical Reason: It is a refutation of his previous views. He based his religion not on pure reason but on morals. Ethical obligation is a reality.

The Critique of Judgement: In this book, Kant finds God in the beautiful design of nature based on "patterns laid up in the heavens. The layman feels the presence of God in the two great mysteries 'the starry heavens above and the law within'."

Importance of Education

He wrote, "Man can become only through education".

Aim of Education

Kant wrote, "Children should be educated not with reference to present condition of things, but rather with regard to a possibly improved state of the human race—that is according to the ideal of humanity and its entire destiny and perfection which consist in absolute moral worth".

Guidelines for Moral Education

Prof. Marlow Ediger has summarised Kant's guidelines in stressing morality as under:

1. Morality should stress universals in space and time. Moral guidelines are not specific but flexible such as the Golden Rule. Flexibility in implementing the Golden Rule makes moral generalisations applicable to any place or region on the face of the earth, as well as applicable in any period of time. The time of application could be in the past, present, or future.
2. Morality in its manifestations may not bring happiness necessarily to the personal self. It could be painful to apply the Golden Rule. Certainly, just acts and deeds may not always bring contentment to the doer.
3. It is a duty to treat others as ends and not as means to an end. Duty is different from desire or wish.
4. Each person has the freedom to choose. Hopefully, ethical rather than unethical values will be chosen. Each person then possesses free will.
5. Individuals are entirely responsible for their choices whether they be moral or immoral.
6. Human beings are born as being good individuals. However, wrong decisions can be made pertaining to the unethical and the immoral.
7. Students must be taught to be thinking, reasoning individuals. The goal in education is to develop the moral being.
8. Self-discipline is necessary to curb the undesirable choices and decisions in life.
9. Human nature is improved through education and schooling.

10. Cultivation of the mind or intellect is a major goal of education. The intellect must develop into a being who is able to think critically, as well as analyse information.
11. Individuals need to emphasise the concept of wisdom when developing the rational powers.
12. Predictions in science do not interfere in the decision making arena. Cause and effect then is not involved in reasoning and in thinking.
13. Kant's *Critique of Practical Reason* states that the individual makes choices and decisions in the ethical domain. In his *Critique of Pure Reason,* Kant emphasises that nature stresses causes and effects.

10

John Henrich Pestalozzi

(1746-1827)

Pestalozzi, a great Swiss educator was born at Zurich in 1746. His father, a physician, passed away when he was just five years old. He was brought up by his mother who encouraged his sensitivity. He hated the Latin school at Zurich as it lacked realism. He, however, enjoyed his college years at the *Collegium Humanitatis* and *Collegium Carolinum*.

Pestalozzi tried several professions including law and politics but ultimately took up agriculture and developed a farm at Neuh. During his work at the farm, he began his first experiments in education. He started to educate his own child, Jacobi, in the manner of Emile but soon made some modifications. He wrote, "To have a knowledge of words with no distinct idea of the things they represent enormously increases the difficulty of getting at the truth... Teach him nothing by words that you can teach him by things themselves. Nature teaches him better than men. Remember that if restraint robs you of your pupil's confidence, all your labour is lost".

Pestalozzi turned his farmhouse into a shelter for destitute children. He thought that their natural need to be active and inborn powers would lead to self-support at an early age. He, therefore, combined education, moral regeneration and practical training in agriculture and handicrafts. He taught the children by means of conversation on all kinds of topics. This farm and consequently school at the farm had to be closed on account of financial difficulties.

Pestalozzi's work at Neuh and Stanz where he was in charge of poor children convinced him that a new approach to education was needed.

Pestalozzi set up a school at Burgdorf and a boarding school at yerdun where he conducted his educational experiments. The school with its natural and relaxed environment ran harmoniously and attracted attention of educators. His method of instruction was greatly appreciated.

A letter of appreciation from the school examiners/inspectors reflects his work: "All that you hoped from your method of teaching has been realised. You have shown that what powers already exist in even the youngest child, in what way are these powers to be developed, and how each talent must be sought out and exercised in such a way as to bring it to maturity. The astonishing progress made by your young pupils in spite of their many differences of character and disposition, clearly shows that every child is good for something, when the master knows how to find out his talents, and cultivate them in a truly psychological manner. Your teaching has brought to light the foundations on which all instructions must be based, if it is ever to be of any real use; it also shows that from the tender age, and in a very short time, a child's mind can attain a wonderful breadth of development which must make its influence felt, not only during his few years of study, but throughout his whole life".

Publications

Pestalozzi's views on education are contained in his following publications:

1. *Evening Hours of a Hermit*
2. *Leonard and Gertrude*
3. *How Gertrude Teaches Her Children*
4. *The Swan Song*
5. *Letters on Early Education*

In his *Evening Hours of Hermit*, Pestalozzi explained his ideas in three ways—as a practical educational reformer, through his philosophical and sociological thought.

Like Rousseau's *Emile,* Pestalozzi's *Leonard and Gertrude* is written in the style of a novel. However, the difference between the two is striking. While Rousseau dreamt of social isolation, Pestalozzi presented his story in a Swiss village, with complete absorption in the life and grief of poor fellow men. Gertrude represents the living symbol of the 'road of nature'. He wrote, "Nature, herself, bids a man to look to his own interests and those of his family".

In *How Gertrude Teaches Her Children,* Pestalozzi provides a systematic psychological theory of his educational method. He says, "The mechanism of physical human nature is essentially subject to the same laws by which physical nature generally unfolds her powers. According to these laws, all instruction should graft the most essential parts of its subjects firmly into the very being of the human mind; then join the same essential parts of its subjects firmly into the very being of the human mind; then join the less essential gradually but uninterruptedly to the most essential, and maintain all the parts of the subject, even to the outermost, in one living, proportionate whole".

Gertrude, the pious mother of the children of the village where Leonard lived, brought about the regeneration of the village, primarily through education. The method of instruction was very simple. She gave them instruction in the rudiments of arithmetic with daily exercises. She taught them to count the number of steps from one end of the room to the other. Two of the rows of five panels each, in one of the windows gave her an opportunity to unfold the decimal relations of numbers. She also made them count their threads while spinning. She taught how to observe the forces of nature carefully and intelligently.

How Gertrude Teaches Her Children is a sort of manual to the mothers. It contains exercises for children. It also provides a systematic theory of his methods.

Pestalozzi also wrote 'Fables' with a Moral

Luella Cole in *A History of Education – Socrates to Montessori* has given an account of Pestalozzi's work with pre-school children. In the course of his work, it occurred to him that the task of educating a child inevitably began with the mother who could use the pre-school years to better purpose than was often the case, so that children might arrive at school age already in possession of simple facts and skills. The time thus saved would permit teachers to give a more advanced education during the school years than was possible when the children had no training before entrance in the lowest class. In his book he set forth a number of exercises some of which are certainly too hard for pre-school children".

Main Educational Ideas and Practices Propounded

1. *Meaning of Education*: "Education is the natural progressive

and harmonious development of all the powers and capacities of human beings".

In *Swan Song* Pestalozzi wrote, "The education of all three sides of our nature procedes on common lines in equal measure".

2. *Direct Method of Acquiring Knowledge*: Pestalozzi named his direct method of acquiring knowledge an *Anschauung*. This means that the child acquires knowledge by his own experience. He observed, "I wish to psychologise education".

The function of instruction is to remove the confusion of the first impression. This implies:

(i) Separating the objects from one another to make them distinct.

(ii) Putting together in imagination those which are related to each other to make them all clear to children.

(iii) Putting across in children clear ideas through proper explanation.

3. *Model of the School*: Pestalozzi stressed that the school should follow the model of the home. Let the teacher act like a father. He should set an example in all activities. Just as cooperation and mutual understanding govern a good house, so these ideals should be applied to the school.

4. *Sense Perception*: He was a believer in the value of sense impressions for learning. He said, "Man's knowledge must be founded on sense impression".

5. *Medium of Play*: Pestalozzi believed that children express their natural drives through play.

6. *Discipline*: According to Pestalozzi, the children's trust in their teachers, their love and gratitude for them should take the place of rules and discipline.

7. *Vocational Education*: Pestalozzi emphasised the necessity of vocational education.

8. *Three Well-marked Stages in the Development of Mind*:

(i) The mind first begins with impressions. Gradually impressions become distinct and take individual forms as units of experience.

(ii) At the next stage, sense impressions become clear. The form and other qualities of things are imagined by the mind.

(iii) At the last stage, the clear images of things are transformed into ideas by which things can be understood clearly.

9. *Curriculum*: Activities at Yverdun schools included drawing, writing, singing, physical exercises, group recitations, model making, collecting map making and field trips.

Lower Class			Upper Class		
Sl. No.	*Curriculum*	*Hrs.*	*Sl. No.*	*Curriculum*	*Hrs.*
1.	Nature Study	2	1.	Natural history	2
2.	Description of products of art	2	2.	Technical work	2
3.	Geography	2	3.	Arithmetic	6
4.	Knowledge of the country (walking)	2	4.	Geometry and Drawing	4
5.	Mental arithmetic	6	5.	Language	4
6.	Drawing	4	6.	Singing	3
7.	Reading and language	6	7.	Religion	9
8.	Singing	3			
9.	Religion	6			
	Total	33		**Total**	30

There were three classes – primary, lower and upper – primary for children under 8, lower for between 8 and 11 and upper primary for 11 to 18.

10. *Ability Grouping*: The students were divided into ability grouping according to individual differences.

11. *Teacher Training*: Pestalozzi introduced teacher training at Yverdun school. Educators were attracted from Europe and America to study the working of this institution. They were so impressed that they started several schools for the training of teachers in their countries.

'Anschauung' of Pestalozzi

Meaning of Anschauung. There is no precise equivalent English word to *Anschauung. Anschauung* is a method of instruction teaching by experience. Usually following terms are used to convey the meaning of this concept—concrete experience, direct acquaintance, direct experience, first hand impression, personal contact experience, face to face knowledge and direct impact of persons and things. *Anschauung* may be described as: "The relations and proportions of number and form constitute the natural measures of all those impressions which the mind receives from without. They comprehend the qualities of the material world; form being the measure of space, and number the measure of time". He distinguished three aspects of *Anschauung,* namely, form, number and name.

Three-fold Principles

1. Principle of teaching children to look upon every object that is brought before them as a unit, that is separated from those with which it is connected.
2. Principle of teaching children the form of every object that is, its size and proportions.
3. Principle of recency so as to make children immediately acquainted with all the words and names descriptive of objects known to them.

Techniques of Instruction

(a) He emphasised that the techniques of instruction should be directed to the primary faculties of counting, measuring and speaking which lie at the basic of accurate knowledge of objects of sense.

(b) Appreciation of form was developed by Pestalozzi mainly through drawing on the basis that children are ready at an early age for getting knowledge of proportion and for using slate and pencil in making tiny letters.

(c) For language teaching, he reduced language to words or names.

Pestalozzi described his method of teaching arithmetic in these words: "For instance, when he asked in arithmetic—How many times is seven contained in sixty-three? The child has no real background for his answer, and must with great difficulty dig it out of his memory. Now, by the plan of putting nine times seven objects before his eyes, and letting him count them as nine sevens standing together, he has not to think anymore about this question; he knows from what he has already learnt, although he is asked for the first time, that seven is contained nine times in sixty-three. So it is in other subjects—this is my method". Pestalozzi explains the general principle of *Anschauung* as applied to arithmetic in these words: "That by exercising children beginning to count with real objects, or at least with dots representing them, we lay the foundation of the whole of the science of arithmetic, and secure their future progress from error and confusion.

Regarding the teaching of language, Pestalozzi wrote, "I always put the picture before the eye, then sought for a word, for the picture".

Major Contributions

1. All round and harmonious development as the aim of education.
2. Maximum freedom to the learner.
3. Analytic method of teaching.
4. Objects to come before symbols.
5. Play as the medium.
6. Stress on correlation.
7. Teacher training.
8. Ability grouping.
9. Concept of *Anschauung*.

Limitations of Pestalozzi's Educational Ideas and Practices

1. He insisted on beginning instruction with the elements of experiences but did not provide a definite idea of the elements of experiences.
2. His method of instruction was not suitable for advanced stages of learning.
3. There was no definite curriculum. Instruction was at random. Instruction was done on disconnected topics.

Some views on the His Contribution to Education Thought and Practices

Carroll Atkinson and Eurgene T. Maleska in *The Story of Education* (1962):

"Pestalozzi insisted that the natural instincts of a child should provide the motives for learning. He considered cooperation and sympathy, rather than compulsion or physical punishment, the proper means by which to achieve discipline. Influenced by Rousseau, he believed that free expression would allow the natural powers of child to develop. Since it is nature that gives the drive to life, he maintained that the teacher's responsibility is to adapt instruction to each individual according to his particular changing, unfolding nature as required at the various stages of his development. Pestalozzi looked upon the child as a unity made of moral, physical, and intellectual powers—all of which could be developed harmoniously through education."

Marlow Ediger of the Northern Missouri University, USA has summarised the views of Pestalozzi as under:

1. Reality rather than abstractions should be in evidence in the school curriculum in initial student learning.
2. The semi-concrete (models and illustrations) should follow realistic concrete experiences.
3. Students should master each step of learning prior to progressing to the next ordered activity or experience.
4. Physical punishment of pupils, in general, should be eliminated discipline based on love should be experienced by all students.
5. The use of the senses in learning is vital. These senses include the traditional utilization of touch, smell, taste, hearing, and sight. Developing the senses in learning should receive paramount emphasis.

Pestalozzi would definitely oppose:

1. Rote learning of content without students understanding what has been learned.
2. Drill and practice without developing pupil interest in ongoing activities and experiences.
3. Survey approaches in teaching-learning situations without students attaining content in depth.
4. Physical punishment of students without emphasizing students enjoying ongoing activities and experiences.

5. Forced discipline upon pupils without developing spontaneous quality behaviour within students.

The only way to correct misunderstanding between teacher and pupil, according to Pestalozzi, was for the teacher to commence with sense impressions of the object of the lesson. Only after time for these impressions to take effect had elapsed should the teacher proceed to the naming of the object. Once named, the object could be studied as to its form; that is, its various qualities could be discussed and compared. Finally, with the abstractions of its essential as against its accidental qualities, the object was ready for definition. This, in brief, is what Pestalozzi so frequently refers to as the essence of his method, teaching everything through number, form, and language. In this way language and observation or experience are always so closely linked that education should henceforth be well on its way to eliminating forever rote memory without comprehension.

To sum up the great German Philosopher Fichte had observed that the type of education developed by Pestalozzi would regenerate the nation. What Pestalozzi contributed to education throughout the world was a basic idea that 'Education consists of guiding children into a natural and orderly unfolding of their innate capacities'.

R. Rusk finds the following salient features of Pestalozzi's work:

1. *Anschauung* – the common starting point of all instruction.
2. Pestalozzi insistence that teaching should follow an orderly sequence.
3. Formulation of 'a method' based on psychological principles.
4. Recognition of the practical and emotional aspects of personality.
5. Laying the basis of elementary school system.
6. Reinforcing democratic tradition in education.

11

Frederich August Froebel
(1782-1852)

Froebel, the founder of the Kindergarten was born on April 21, 1782 in Oberweiback, a village in South Germany. He lost his mother when he was just nine months old. His father remarried when Froebel was only four years of age. His father was indifferent towards him and his step mother's treatment was very unfair. Thus he was deprived of parental affection, love and care. At the age of eleven he was adopted by his uncle who was associated with a church near his village. In school, he was considered as a dunce.

At the age of fourteen, he became an apprentice to a forester. It was here that he developed a deep love for nature and acquired the habits of observation and concentration which characterised him throughout his life.

At seventeen, he joined the University of Jena where he was profoundly influenced by the idealistic philosophy of Fitche and Schelling. On account of financial difficulty, he discontinued his studies.

For four years, he remained a 'career-wanderer'. He wandered from place to place, picking up professions of different nature and failing miserably in them, one after the other.

Interest in Education

A turning point came in the life of Froebel when he began to study architecture at Frankfurt. There he came in contact with Dr. Grunner who was the Director of a model school. Dr. Grunner discovered that Froebel had the potential to become an excellent teacher and persuaded him to join his school. This marked a turning point in his life. Froebel was greatly satisfied and he found his 'long missed life element' and was 'inexpressibly happy'. He declared, for the first time "I found something I had always longed for, but always missed, as if my life had at last discovered its native element; I felt as happy as a fish in the water or a bird in the air".

After spending three years at Frankfurt, Froebel paid a visit to Pestalozzi's institute at Yverdun. There Froebel learnt in detail the principles and method of Pestalozzi. Froebel's contact with Pestalozzi prepared him for carrying out his own experiments which led to the founding of his own school.

In 1816, Froebel established a small school at Griesheim which later on was shifted to Keilhau. In this school, Froebel developed his own principles and methods of instruction. After passing through several vicissitudes, this school became a successful institution in a period of ten years. 'Play' and 'art work' were the chief features of this school.

Publication of *The Education of Man*

In 1826, Froebel published his famous book *The Education of Man*. In this he says: "The true method of education consists in considering the mind of the child as a whole in which all the parts work together to produce harmonious unity". After this he started many schools in Germany. The Government suspected the revolutionary ideas of Froebel and an enquiry was conducted. The inspector gave a favourable report: "I found here a closely united family of some sixty members held together in mutual confidence and every member seeking the good of the whole – The aim of institution is by no means knowledge and science merely, but free self-active development of the mind from within".

Froebel's Work

On account of financial difficulties, Froebel shifted his work to Switzerland in 1830. The Swiss Government appreciated his work and sent teachers for training under him. He then moved to Burgdorf. There he became a superintendent of an orphanage. He continued his work of training teachers. There he realised that due to non-availability of education in the pre-school age, the school suffered and did not get good raw material – the educand.

Froebel returned to Germany in 1836 and founded his first kindergarten in 1849 in the village of Blankendurg. He married his kindergartener in 1849. He spent his whole time in the founding and devising his apparatus for kindergartens.

His views were not accepted by the German Government and forbade him from establishing any school. This was a great shock, he could not survive long and died in 1852, in poverty, misery and agony. His grave is marked by a slab with a cube, a cylinder and a sphere on it.

Main Features of Educational Philosophy and Principles

1. *Object of Education*: In Froebel's own words, "The object of education is the realisation of the faithful, pure, inviolable and hence holy life. The divine essence of man should be unfolded, brought out, lifted into consciousness, and man himself raised into free, conscious, obedience to the divine principle that lives in him and to a free representation of this principle in his life. Education should lead and guide man to clearness concerning himself and in himself, to face with nature, and to unity with God".

Froebel maintains that the aim of education is not to make the mind of the child a jumble of words. He writes: "The essential business of school is not so much to communicate a variety and multiplicity of facts as to give prominence to the ever living unity that is in all things". Again he writes: "Human education requires the knowledge and appreciation of religion, nature and language in their intimate living reciprocity and mutual interaction. Without the knowledge and appreciation of the intimate unity of the three, the school and we ourselves are lost in the fallacies of bottomless, self-provoking diversity." So the aim of education is to enable the child to realise the unity in diversity.

2. *Principle of Development*: Froebel asserts: "Each individual must develop from within, self-active and free, in accordance with the internal law".

3. *Mind of the Child as a Living Whole*: According to Froebel, "The true method of education consists in considering the mind of the child as a living whole in which all the parts work together to produce harmonious unity".

4. *Creativeness of Childhood*: Froebel proposed a new concept of childhood. He stressed that childhood is not merely a preparation for adulthood. Childhood is a value in itself and possesses its own creation. An adult has no right to feel superior and to interfere with the nature of children. Rather the adult must first understand the child and then guide him accordingly.

5. *Inner Relatedness of all Education*: This means that that educator ought to lead the child through such situations as will help to relate his experiences organically one with another. Only then can the child realise his own personal unity and the unity inherent in the diversity of life.

6. *Totality of Educational Endeavour*: In order to realise the driving character of the universe and his part in it, man needs his senses and emotions as well as reasons. They all are windows of the soul. Hence Froebel emphasised the totality of educational endeavour.

7. *Play and Activity*: According to Froebel, "Play is the purest, most important activity of man at this stage. It gives, therefore, joy, freedom, contentment, inner rest and peace with the world. It holds the source of all that is good". Froebel recognised that play needs to be organised and controlled on definite materials so that it may not degenerate into aimless play "instead of preparing for those tasks of life fcr which it is destined".

8. *Freedom to the Child*: The child should be educated in free atmosphere. Freedom means obedience to self-imposed law.

9. *Social Aspect*: Froebel stressed the social aspect of education also. He believed that all social institutions like the home, the school, the church and the State, etc. are the agencies of development of the individual wherein he is to realise the unity in diversity.

10. *Importance of Songs*: He devised songs, gestures and construction as the chief means of stimulating the imagination of the child.

11. *Role of the Teacher*: The teacher is like a gardener who carefully nurses and protects children in order to secure their full and free development along most desirable lines. The educator by his efforts assists the educand who is developing according to the law of his nature to attain levels that would be denied to him.

Kindergarten: Meaning, Objective and Environment

Meaning of the Kindergarten: Kindergarten is a German word which means a children's garden. Froebel conceived the school as a garden, the teacher as the gardener and the students as tender plants. The teacher, like the gardener, looks after the little human plants and waters them to grow to beauty and perfection. Froebel discovered great similarity between a child and a plant. He believed that the process of growth and development of the plant and the child is the same. The plant grows from within according to the seed that is within. In the same way the child grows from within. He unfolds his tendencies and impulses from within.

Objective of the Kindergarten: In the words of Froebel, "The objective of a kindergarten is to give the children employment in agreement with their whole nature, to strengthen their bodies, to exercise their senses, to engage their awakening mind and through their senses to make them acquainted with nature and their fellow creatures. It is specially to guide the heart and the affections, and to lead them to the original ground of all life, to unity with themselves".

Environment of the Kindergarten: The environment of the kindergarten is to be that of freedom, play and joy - an environment which fosters self-expression. There are to be no books or fixed intellectual tasks for children, but training in expression is to be given in three ways - songs, movements and construction. These three are to go together. Though the means are separate yet the process is connected as a whole, e.g., when a story is told or read, it is expressed in song, dramatised in movement and gesture, and illustrated by construction from blocks, paper, clay or drawing. Thus the child's imagination and thought are encouraged and stimulated by concerted means. His hands and limbs, his eyes and other senses are trained by making him do certain things.

Characteristics of Kindergarten

1. *Free Self-Activity*: Froebel regarded self-activity as a process by which the individual realises his own nature and builds up his own world and then unites and harmonises the two. An inspector reported about this self-activity: "Self-activity of the mind is the first law of this institution, the kind of instruction given here does not make the young mind a strong box into which, as early as possible kinds of coins of the most different values and coinage, such as are now current in the world that are stuffed, but slowly, continuously, gradually and always inwardly that is according to a connection found in nature of the human mind, the instruction steadily goes on without any

ticks, from the simple to the complex, from the concrete to the abstract, so well-adapted to the child and his needs that he goes as easily to his learning as to his play".

The following points should be noted regarding activity:

(i) It should not be vague.

(ii) It should be a sublimated or controlled activity.

(iii) Social atmosphere is essential in order to secure meaningful activities.

(iv) Self-activity may take the form either of work or of play.

2. *Play*: According to Froebel, "Play is the purest, most spiritual activity of man at this stage. ... It gives, therefore, joy, freedom, contentment, inner rest and peace with the world. It holds the source of all that is good". Froebel recognised that play needs to be organised and controlled on definite materials so that it may not degenerate into aimless play instead of preparing for those tasks of life for which it is destined". There should be rational conscious guidance. Consequently, Froebel has given seven gifts to children to play with.

3. *Songs, Gestures and Construction*: Froebel saw an organic relationship between songs, gestures and construction. He regarded these as three coordinate forms of expression in the child. What is to be learnt by the pupil is first expressed in a song, then it is dramatised or expressed in gesture or movement and lastly illustrated through some constructive work such as paper or clay. Thus, a balanced development of the mind, the speech organs and the hand is aimed at. These three activities provide exercise to the senses, limbs and muscles of the child.

4. *Gifts and Occupations*: For providing appropriate activities, Froebel devised suitable materials known as gifts. The gifts suggest some form of activity and occupations are the activities suggested by gifts. These have been carefully graded. They possess all the novelty of play things. The order of the gift is devised in such a way as it leads the child from the activities and thought of one stage to another.

5. *Role of the Teacher*: The teacher is not a spectator and a passive person. He is expected to suggest suitable occupations when gifts are given to children. He demonstrates certain activities to them. He also sings a song with a view to help the child to form appropriate ideas.

A teacher has important responsibilities to perform. He has to inculcate sympathetically values like love, sympathy, humility, cooperation and obedience to elders.

6. *Positive Discipline*: The teacher has to avoid external restraint and bodily punishment. The child should be made to realise that discipline depends upon his love for order, goodwill and mutual understanding. Froebel stressed that women should be trained for training children at this stage.

7. *Curriculum*: It is in term of activities. The divisions of the curriculum are:

(i) Manual work.
(ii) Religion and religious instruction.
(iii) Natural science and mathematics.
(iv) Language.
(v) Arts and objects of art.

Froebel's Gifts

For the complete education and training of child, Froebel devised a series of gifts. The gifts comprise carefully graduated series of materials which possess all the novelty of playthings, and form the basis of his educational method. They are to train the senses of sight and touch, to give the child an idea of size and surface, and to present him a correct idea of number. The activities suggested by these gifts are called occupations. The gifts are given to the child in a certain order. The gradation and order elements of gifts are determined by the principle of development. The gifts are twenty in number although only the first seven are now usually called by this name.

Gift I

It consists of six coloured woollen balls, three in primary colours, red, yellow and blue, and three secondary colours, orange, green and purple. The occupation consists in rolling them about in play. Thus they develop in the children the idea of colour and material, form, motion, direction and muscular sensibility.

Gift II

It consists of a sphere, cube and cylinder made of hardwood. In playing with these gifts, the child notices the difference between the stability of the cube, and the mobility of the sphere. He observes that the cylinder is both stable and movable, and that it harmonises both the qualities in one.

Gift III

It is a large cube divided into eight smaller equal cubes. From these the child can build up a number of useful artistic forms such as benches, steps, doors, bridges, etc. and for this reason the third gift is often called the *first building box*. The child can also gain elementary ideas of addition and subtraction through these cubes.

Gift IV

It consists of the large cubes divided into eight oblong prisms in each of which the length is twice the breadth and the breadth is twice the thickness. This helps the child to construct different kinds of buildings and patterns when combined with the third gift.

Gift V

It is every much like the third gift. It consists of a large cube divided into twenty-seven small cubes, three of which are again divided diagonally into halves and three into quarters. The child can construct many beautiful forms and patterns by combining the third, fourth and fifth gifts. Form and number can very well be taught by the use of this gift.

Gift VI

It is again similar to gift four. In it there is a large cube divided into eighteen whole and nine small oblong blocks. Still further designs in forms and construction may be made by the child. It is also useful in teaching numbers.

Gift VII

It is also a set of square and triangular tablets made of fine wood in two colours. It provides material for several exercises in geometrical forms and mosaic work.

Other gifts consist of materials such as stick-laying, perforating, paper-cutting, threading of beads, mat-making, embroidery, basket-making, wire work, drawing and modelling.

Play-Way Method

Froebel used play for the development and growth of the child in the kindergarten established by him. This method came to be known as the play-way method in teaching-learning.

Play-Way is thus a method which envisages that all work should be done in the spirit of play. Play-Way is quite different from the normal meaning of the word play which is considered as a form of physical activity. Play-Way, on the other hand, is a means for the cognitive, and affective development of the child, *i.e.*, development of intellect, skills and feelings.

Principles of Play-Way Method

1. Principle of growth and development of the child through play.
2. Principle of self-development under teacher's guidance.
3. Principle of self-activity.
4. Principle of self-expression through play.
5. Principle of spontaneity.
6. Principle of freedom.
7. Principle of happiness and joy in play activities.
8. Principle of unity.
9. Principle of aesthetic appreciation.
10. Principle of creativeness.
11. Principle of drawing out.
12. Principle of discipline through love.
13. Principle of sense training.
14. Principle of concrete to abstract.

Gifts, Occupations, Songs, Gestures and Construction in the Play-Way

We have already stressed the place of activity and play. To provide activities, Froebel devised suitable materials known as gifts. The gifts suggest some form of activity and occupations are the activities suggested by gifts. These have been carefully graded. They possess all the novelty of play things. The order of the gift is devised in such a way as it leads the child from the activities and thought of one stage to another. Froebel saw an organic relationship between play, songs, gestures and construction.

Play-Way Activities Connected with Songs

Selection of Songs. Froebel has given songs in his book *Mother and Nursery Songs.* There are fifty play songs. The idea of the introduction of songs is to enable the child to use his senses, limbs and muscles and also to familiarise him with the surroundings. The child begins to use language through these songs. Each song is accompanied by a game such as 'Hide and Seek'. The selection of the song is determined by the teacher in accordance with the development of the child. There are three parts in a song.

1. A motto for the guidance of mother or teacher.
2. A verse accompanied by music.
3. A picture illustrating the song.

The song for drill is:

Let us have a drill to-day,
    March along grand array,
And whoever steps the best,
    Shall be captain over the rest,
And lead us on our way.

Play-Way Activities Based on Gifts and Educational Objectives

Some Examples:

	Educational Objective	*Components of the Gift*	*Activity*
1.	Enabling the child to learn the concept of colour, form, motion, direction, and muscular sensitivity.	Six coloured balls of different colours.	Children are required to roll these balls in play-way attitude of mind.
2.	Enabling the stu-dents to learn the concept of sta-bility and mobility and to differentiate between these two.	One sphere. One cube. One cylinder – made of hard wood.	Children are required to observe the stability and mobility of each article while playing.
3.	Enabling the students to learn the concepts of addition and subtraction.	One large cube divided into eight smaller equal cubes contained in a box.	Children are required to build a number of forms, e.g., benches, doors, etc.

	Educational Objective	*Components of the Gift*	*Activity*
4.	Enabling children to develop concepts of designs or patterns.	A large cube divided into eight oblong prisms. Each has a length twice its brea-dth and breadth twice its thickness.	Children are occupied in the building of a variety of patterns by using these prisms.
5.	Enabling the children to develop the concepts of form and number through gifts 3, 4 and 5.	Gift 5 consists of a large cube divided into 27 small cubes. Three of these are sub-divided diago-nally into haves; three further sub-divi-ded into haves; three further subdivided into quarters.	Children are occupied in developing a variety of forms using gifts 3, 4 and 5.
6.	Enabling the children to develop the concept of numbers.	Large cubes divided into eighteen wholes and nine small oblong bricks (Like gift 4).	Children are directed to develop designs using the material of the gift.
7.	Enabling the children to acquire the concept of mosaic and geometrical forms.	A set of triangular and square tablets of fine wood in two different colours.	Children are directed to prepare geometrical forms and mosaic work.

Role of the Teacher

The teacher plays the role of a gardener who looks after the tender plants. He provides an environment of life and freedom. He plans his work very carefully and demonstrates the play-way activity. He always keeps in mind the chief objectives which the gifts and songs should serve.

Merits of Play-Way Method

1. It stresses the importance of play in early education.

2. The gifts and occupations of the Kindergarten give a new approach to method of teaching.
3. The inclusion of creative work in the school makes children creative workers.
4. There is sufficient scope for activity in a Kindergarten.
5. Various gifts provide sensory training.
6. The inclusion of nature study in the curriculum helps to develop love for nature and the world in the mind of the students.

Limitations of Play-Way Method

1. In the Kindergarten, too much stress is laid on the development from within.
2. Songs as given by Froebel are out of date. These cannot be used in every school.
3. The gifts of Froebel are formal in nature.
4. The order of presentation of gifts is arbitrary.
5. They do not serve much purpose of sense training.
6. There is little of correlation in the teaching of various subjects.
7. It is not possible to accept his excessive emphasis on play in education as it is likely to detract the child from serious learning.
8. Philosophy on which Froebel based his method is very complicated. It is very difficult for children to understand his symbolism.

Contribution to Educational Thought and Principles

Froebel has made a very valuable contribution to educational theory and practice. Froebel's Play-Way finds place in the teaching-learning process at all stages of education and in all subjects. Following are the important elements which are emphasised by modern educators and thinkers:

1. *Respect for the Child's Individuality*: Froebel lived for children, worked for children and died for children. He had profound love and sympathy for children.

2. *Emphasis on the Study of the Child*: Froebel stressed the need for the study of the nature of the child, his instincts and impulses. Modern educator is very careful to see that adequate scope is

provided for the free play of the impulses and instincts of children.

3. *Education Through Play*: Froebel believed that play is the highest phase of self-development. He introduced Play-Way in the activities of the school. Today we find that the principle of Play-Way has been accepted by every educator. We teach children through songs, movements, gestures, dramatisation, hand-work, etc.

4. *Activity in Education*: Froebel was the first educator to make self-activity as the basis of education. 'Learning by doing' is the slogan of the day.

5. *Sense Training*: Froebel introduced gifts for the training of the senses of children. With the help of these gifts, he wanted to give the idea of shape, form, colour, size and number. Audio-visual aids form an integral part of the present system of education.

6. *Nature Study in Education*: For Froebel, nature study was a means of bringing the child nearer God. He advocated nature study to enable the child to understand the world in which he lives and to develop habits of careful observation. This idea has become so popular that we do not regard any school worthy of name if it does not provide for nature study.

7. *Women Teachers at the Nursery Stage*: It will not be wrong to say that it is due to the influence of Froebel that we find a trend to entrust the education at the pre-primary or pre-basic stage to women teachers who are considered to be more suited for this task of instruction at this stage.

8. *Stress on Nursery or Pre-Primary Education:* The present educator fully recognises the importance of the education in the early years. Today we find a large number of schools catering to the needs of such children. Froebel often said, "Until the education of nursery years was reformed nothing solid and worthy could be achieved."

9. *New Conception of School:* His kindergarten school was a little world where responsibility was shared, by all, individual-rights respected by all, brotherly sympathy developed and voluntary co-operation practised. His school was an ideal society in miniature.

Froebel's Eternal Message

'Come! Let us live for Children".

12

Abraham Lincoln

(1809-1865)

From log cabin (a sort of small hut) to the White House (Presidential Residence) is the real life history of Abraham Lincoln to become the President of the USA (1861-1865). Abraham's father was a farmer and carpenter. Since his childhood, Lincoln was fond of reading, and constantly borrowed books from his neighbours. Lincoln became a successful attorney. He became known to the institution of slavery. In 1846, he became a member of the United States House of Representatives and in 1861 he became the 16th US President.

Educational Thoughts

The following extracts from the letter which he wrote to the headmaster of a school in which his son was studying indicates his views on education.

He will have to learn, I know, that all men are not just, all men are not true. But teach him also that for every scoundrel there is a hero; that for every selfish politician, there is a dedicated leader.

Teach him that for every enemy there is a friend. It will take time, I know, but teach him if you can, that a dollar earned is of more value than five pound.

Teach him learn to lose and also to enjoy winning.

Steer him away from envy, if you can.

Teach him the secret of quiet laughter.

Let him learn early that the bullies are the easiest to lick.

Teach him, if you can, the wonder of books, but also give him quiet time to ponder over the external mystery of birds in the sky, bees in the sun, and flowers on a green hill-side.

In school, teach him it is far more honourable to fail than to cheat.

Teach him to have faith in his own ideas, even if everyone tells him they are wrong.

Teach him to be gentle with gentle people and tough with the tough.

Try to give my son the strength not to follow the crowd when everyone is getting on the band wagon.

Teach him to listen to all men but teach him also to filter all he hears on a screen of truth and take only the good that comes through.

Teach him, if you can, how to laugh when he is sad.

Teach him, there is no shame in tears.

Teach him to scoff at cynics and to beware of too much sweetness.

Teach him to sell his brawn and brain to the highest bidders; but never to put a price tag on his heart and soul.

Teach him to close his ears to a howling mob, and to stand and fight if he thinks he is right.

Teach him gently, but do not cuddle him because only the test of fire makes fine steel.

Let him have the courage to be impatient, let him have the patience to be brave.

Teach him always to have sublime faith in himself because he will always have sublime faith in mankind.

This is a big order; but see what you can do. He is such a little fellow, my son."

Significant Quotes

Those who deny freedom to others, deserve it not for themselves; and, under a just God, can not long retain it. (*The Collected Works of Abraham Lincoln* edited by Roy P. Basler, Volume III, "Letter To Henry L. Pierce and Others (April 6, 1859), p. 376).

"As I would not be a slave, so I would not be a master. This expresses my idea of democracy". (*Ibid*, Vol. II, p. 532)

"Let us have faith that right makes might, and in that faith, let us, to the end, dare to do our duty as we understand it". (*Lincoln's Coper Institute Address*, February 27, 1860)

"All men are created free and equal". (*Ibid*, Vol. II, p. 502)

"With malice towards none, with charity for all, with firmness in the right as God gives us to see the right, let us strive on to finish the work we are in; to bind up the nation's wounds; to care for him who shall have borne the battle, and for his widow and his orphan—to do all which may achieve and cherish a just and lasting peace, among ourselves, and with all nations". (*Lincoln's Second Inaugural Address*, March 4, 1865)

"The probability that we may fall in the struggle ought not to deter us from the support of a cause we believe to be just; it shall not deter me". (*Ibid* Vol. I, p. 178)

"Leave nothing for tomorrow which can be done today". (*Ibid*, Vol. II, p.81)

"The dogmas of the quiet past are inadequate to the stormy present. As our case is new, so we must think anew, and act anew". (*Lincoln's Second Annual Message to Congress*, December, 1862)

13

Herbert Spencer

(1820-1903)

Herbert Spencer, an English philosopher, is known for scientific trend in education. He was born in Derby. His father was a learned teacher of chemistry and physics. He made suitable arrangement for the education of his child at home. Spencer's natural inclination was towards original thinking. He showed a keen interest in performing experiments in natural sciences and mathematics. He acquired a good deal of knowledge in all subjects while he was just seventeen. His first interest was biology, but he turned to engineering. From 1837 to 1846, he worked as an engineer for the London and Birmingham Railway. Later he served as editor of the Economist. Spencer left the *Economist* in 1853 to pursue his philosophical career. He gained a wide reputation as a philosopher.

Publications

1. *The Principles of Psychology* (1855)
2. *Education* (1861)
3. *First Principles* (1862)
4. *The Principles of Biology* (1864-1867)
5. *The Principles of Ethics* (1892-93)
6. *The Principle of Sociology* (1896)

Contribution to Education

Spencer held that the aim of education was 'to prepare us for complete living'. For complete living one must know how to develop one's body and mind, how to manage one's affairs.

How to manage one's affairs implies:

(i) To bring up a family.
(ii) To behave like a good citizen.
(iii) To utilise leisure profitably.

(iv) To utilise one's whole capacity for one's own and social welfare.

Maxims of Teaching

Spencer has given us the following maxims of teaching:

1. From simple to complex.
2. From known to unknown.
3. From indefinite to definite.
4. From concrete to abstract.
5. From empirical to rational.

Scientific Humanism in Education

Spencer is considered as one of the most important propounders of scientific humanism in education.

Main Features of Scientific Humanism

Scientific humanism has the following characteristics:

1. Scientific humanism rejects all supernatural powers.
2. Scientific humanism opposes all fatalist theories.
3. Scientific humanism gives reasoning the primary importance.
4. Scientific humanism believes in change.
5. Matter and energy exist independently. They do not owe their existence to mind.
6. Humanism believes that man has the immense potential to solve his own problems on the basis of reasoning and analytical power.
7. According to humanism, within certain objective limits, man is the master of his own destiny.
8. Scientific humanism believes in ethics as the moving spirit behind earthly human relations and experiences.
9. Scientific humanism believes in raising the material standard of living of all people.
10. Scientific humanism stands for the welfare of the society.
11. Scientific humanism emphasises democratic values.
12. Scientific humanism believes in the international economic order.

Curriculum

Spencer gave first priority to subjects like physiology, hygiene, physics and chemistry and placed history, politics and economics at the other end of the curriculum.

According to Spencer, science is the key which opens the locks of the knowledge of other subjects. He said, "History cannot be utilised properly without the knowledge of science".

Spencer observed that science introduced the element of utility. There was no work and vocation which could be learnt without the help of science. Spencer was of the view that the knowledge of science was essential for preparing us for life.

Moral Training

Spencer laid stress on the moral behaviour of the parents for moral training of the children. He believed in the 'theory of natural consequences' as emphasised by Rousseau.

14

Leo Tolstoy

(1828-1910)

Tolstoy, a Russian educator-cum novelist has made a unique contribution to educational thinking. His fame as a novelist has to some extent obscured his writings on education. His writings are based on his first hand experiences.

In 1849, at the age of 21, Tolstoy opened a school on his ancestral estate at Yasnaya Polyana, for the education of peasant children but was not successful. During 1851 to 1856, he served in the army. After retirement from army he, once more took up teaching at his native place with a large number of peasant children. With a view to gain more knowledge on the various dimensions of teaching, he visited several countries of Europe including France, Germany and Switzerland during 1857 to 1862.

Tolstoy was keenly interested in restructuring the national system of education in Russia. In the 1870s, he worked on the compilation of school textbooks. Gandhiji was greatly impressed by his work on education.

War and Peace is the monumental work of Tolstoy.

Educational Thought

In his first book *The Four Periods of Development* he described the process by which human character is formed from early childhood to youth. He highlighted the need for a respectful attitude towards the child's personality and this idea became the cornerstone of his educational work.

Freedom in School

Tolstoy called freedom 'the one and only criterion of education'. On account of this, he is compared with Rousseau. He said that a child is by nature a perfect and innocent creature whose free development should not be hindered. Tolstoy's concept of freedom is explained by Prof. Semion Filippovitch Yegoror as under:

"In Tolstoy's view, freedom in education was a gnoseological and moral principle which had to be put into practice; it was the antithesis of authoritarian teaching, and essential for a humane attitude to the pupil and respect for his or her dignity as a human being. Freedom in education was a principle which stemmed from the internal laws of cognitive activity. Cognition could not be other than free. In the absence of that condition, activity, initiative, consistency, system and all the other tenets of traditional, classical education were of no use, lacking meaning and purpose. The more firmly education was based on that law, the more successful and fruitful it was. Knowledge which had been assimilated could not simply be transmitted and could certainly not be thrust on pupils if they did not want it. Pupils had to apply their own efforts and engage in independent cognitive activity. This they could do best of all by not being forced by a teacher but guided by their own free will".

Holistic View of Child Study

The chief method of child study for Tolstoy was that of many-sided analysis, covering psychological as well as sociological aspects.

Functioning of Yasnaya Polyana School Opened by Tolstoy

The school catered to the boys and girls from 7 to 13. L.N. Tolstoy, Son of Leo Tolstoy describes the chief features of the school in these words:

> "Lessons began between 8 and 9 o'clock in the morning. At noon, there was a break for lunch and a rest. Lessons then continued another three to four hours. Every teacher gave five to six lessons every day. According to their age. readiness and progress, the children were divided into three groups: junior, middle and senior. Pupils did not have places strictly allotted to them. They sat where they liked. No homework was given. The commonest form of educational activity was not the lesson in the usual sense of the word but a free conversation with the pupils during which the children learned reading, writing and arithmetic, their catechism, the rules of grammar, and facts adapted to their

age about history, geography and nature study. They also learned to draw and sing.

"The content of the education given, like its external organisation, was not immutable but changed in accordance with the children's development, the capacities of the school and the teachers, and the wishes of the parents. Tolstoy himself taught mathematics, physics, history and other subjects to the senior group. Most frequently, he told stories in order to teach the fundamentals of science. The children were punished neither for their behaviour nor for poor progress. The requirement that the personality of pupils should be treated with respect pre-supposed that, without punishment or coercion on the part of the adults, they would move towards a recognition of the need to submit to the order on which success at school depended. 'Schoolchildren', said Tolstoy, 'are people, even though they are small. They are people with the same needs as ourselves, who think in the same way as we do. They all want to learn; that is why they go to school and that is why they will have no trouble in understanding that they must submit to certain conditions in order to learn".

Role of the Teachers

The duties of a teacher at Yasnaya Polyana were much more complex than at a school with a strict timetable, coercive discipline, a range of set methods of encouragement and punishment, and a strictly limited volume of knowledge to be studied. Here, the teacher's moral and intellectual faculties were constantly being stretched. They were required at all times to take into consideration of the situation and abilities of each of their charges. In fact, what is known as educational creativity was demanded of the teacher. But the results achieved at the school at Yasnaya Polyana were also different from those at other schools. As a former teacher at Yasnaya Polyana, Yevgeni Markov, said: "We were able to observe the extraordinary progress of Tolstoy's pupils, among whom were some bright little boys who had been taken straight from harrowing or looking after the sheep and after just a few months were able to write quite literate compositions."

Educational Journal 'Yasnaya Polyana'

Tolstoy published this journal primarily with the following objectives:

(a) New educational methods; (b) New principles of administration for people's education; (c) New ways of organising the learning process; (d) Experiments with out-of-school education involving the circulation of books among the people; (e) Monographs describing schools which had come into being spontaneously, with an examination of their achievements and shortcomings, etc.

Tolstoy saw the journal's most important task as studying spontaneous educational activity, throwing light on the underlying links in the process of education, a knowledge of which would be of inestimable value for education as a science and for the teacher as a practitioner. He sought a wide range of contributors to the journal, stipulating only that they must be teachers who looked on their work not only as a means of existence or even as a duty to children, but as a field of experiment to advance the science of education.

Tolstoy himself published articles on the following subjects in the journal:

- People's Education
- Methods of Teaching How to Read and Write
- A Draft Central Plan for the Organisation of People's Schools
- Who Should be Taught to Write and by Whom
- Progress and the Definition of Education

The Tsar authorities (rulers of Russia) did not like the educational views contained in these articles and they considered the journal as 'subverting the fundamental tenets of religion and morality'. Accordingly Tolstoy was prosecuted and the journal ceased publication.

'The Primer'

Tolstoy wrote a textbook for the very young. Its overall plan, content and logical structure were worked out over a prolonged period. Tolstoy was so much excited with this project that he said, "Now I have written the *Primer*, I can die in peace".

Ethical and Moral Teaching

Tolstoy extensively wrote articles on ethical and moral teaching.

Education for All

In the mid-nineteenth century Russia, the majority of the population of the peasants, were still not only uneducated but illiterate. Tolstoy was deeply conscious of the chasm in the society of his time between the cultural achievements and education of the privileged classes and the educational deprivation of the majority of the population. In this tragic division, he saw the source of many social antagonisms and troubles. He felt that education should be available to everyone. If it were made available in equal measure to all sections of the population, it could eliminate despotism and violence, superstition and injustice. "The most pressing need of the Russian people is for education", he declared. (Based on the Article of Semion Filippovitch Yegorov, *Prospects* 24(3/4), 1994)

15

Annie Besant

(1847-1933)

An Irish lady, coming from an aristocratic family, Annie Besant made India her home after coming here in 1893. She became a great lover of Hinduism and claimed that she was a Hindu in her former birth; she wore the Hindu costume and adopted Hindu way of life. She was a great free thinker, a captivating orator and organiser. She was the President of the Theosophical Society of India from 1907 till her death. She played a leading role in the freedom struggle of India and was the President of the Indian National Congress in 1918. Her name is associated with the Home Rule Movement (Movement for Self Rule in India).

Publications

Among her important publications on education, mention may be made of the following:

Education as a National Duty (1903)
The Education of Indian Girls (1906)
Principles of Education (1915)
Education for the New Era (1914)
Theosophical Education Report (1917)

Many-Sided Education

Education according to her should make man a good citizen of free and spiritual commonwealth of humanity. She observed: "What do we find in modern India? An education directed to one part of the body's nature only developing the intelligence, training the intellect, but leaving entirely the spiritual nature and the moral or emotional nature... Such an education can never build up a true man of the world, able to discharge his duties in the world... What sort of nation can you have where the education given to its young is but one quarter what it should be?" Annie Besant describes the all round education in these words: "I look forward to a time when every child shall receive, in the national schools, the elements of a literary, scientific, artistic and technical education. No boy or girl should leave the school ignorant of our literature or of the wonders of science. He should delight in beauty. He should also learn some definite means of breadwinning, let it be tailoring, cookery or any trade or profession. Every pair of hands should be able to do at least some thing well by which an honest living may be earned".

Not Looking for West

Annie Besant wrote: "Let us not look to the West for power in our education. Let us cease to believe that education of the West is the ideal for the East. Far from it, for some parts of the body, we may well go to the West. But for the soul never—only with an education full of Indian unity, full of Indian simplicity, full of Indian purpose, that is of Indian life, can India be herself".

Scheme of Education

According to Annie Besant, following should be the scheme of national education.

1. Education during the first period from birth to seven should be chiefly physical. The body should be given a balanced nutrition in order to secure a healthy development.
2. The second period from seven to fourteen is chiefly emotional. Hence education during this period should be directed towards training and controlling of emotions.
3. Third period from 14-21 years is "the period of rapid intellectual development. Logic and mathematics should be taught intensively. The sense of duty to one's fellowmen should be taught through Civics and Social Studies. Literature, Philosophy and Economics should occupy an important place. Sciences such as Biology, Physiology and Psychology should be mastered. Various aspects of Arts should also be included in the curriculum.

Faith in the Old Gurukula System

She wrote: "Here is an Indian ideal that it would be well to revive. India must have a few representatives (of the ancient *Ashram*) if she is to rise to her former level in supreme intellectual and spiritual achievement". She laid a great stress on the ideal of *Brahmacharya* for a student.

Role of the Teacher

Annie Besant holds that a teacher has to be not only a friend of the body of the child but also of his soul. The teacher must respect the individuality of the child and must not force him into line with his own standard.

Promotion of Women's Education

Annie Besant did a pioneering work in women's education. She organised several groups to strive for the furtherance of girls' schools and colleges in many parts of India where facilities for girl's education did not exist.

Vocational Education

Dr. Besant was a strong advocate for vocational education. Specialisation in some chosen field should prepare the student for his future career in life.

Mother Tongue as the Medium of Instruction

She advocated the use of mother tongue as the medium of instruction. She said, "Nothing denationalises a people as the imposition upon them of a foreign tongue, dominating their life and thought".

Establishment of Educational Institutions and Organisations

She set up organisations like the 'Sons and Daughters of India', 'Scouts and Guides' for inculcating the spirit of selfless service. She formed several schools and colleges. The Central Hindu School and College (Benaras) was established by her in 1898. She launched a plan for the establishment of Benaras Hindu University. Pt. Madan Mohan Malaviya was also a moving figure behind this project.

16
John Dewey
(1859-1952)

Born in October 1859 at Burlington in America, John Dewey was one of the most distinguished educators, philosophers, practitioners and thinkers. After graduating from the University of Vermont in 1879, he started his career as a school teacher. After leaving his job of a school teacher, Dewey joined John Hopkins University and obtained his Ph.D. Degree in Philosophy in 1884. Thereafter for several years, he worked as a Professor of Philosophy at the Universities of Minnesota, Michigan and Chicago. His last assignment was his Professorship of Education and Philosophy at the University of Columbia, New York.

Prof. Dewey delivered lectures on education and philosophy at the University of Peking for a period of two years. The Government of Turkey invited Dewey to draw up a report on the re-organisation of national schools.

His philosophy is not simply speculative but based on actual experiences in the classroom. His principles and practices grew out of his experiments in the University Laboratory School, Chicago. He founded this school in 1896, for the chief objective of testing educational theory through experiments.

Publications

Perhaps no educator has written such a standard and diverse literature on educational principles and practices as Prof. Dewey. Likewise, enormous material has been published on him and his works. His first article entitled *The Metaphysical Assumption of Materialism* appeared in *Journal of Speculative Philosophy* in April 1882. Dewey's important publications are:

1. My Pedagogic Creed (1897), 2. Psychology and Philosophic Method (1899), 3. Studies in Logical Theory (1903), 4. *Ethics* (1908), 5. *The Influence of Darwin and Other Essays* (1910), 6. *How We Think*

(1910), 7. *Democracy and Education* (1916), 8. *Essays in Experimental Logic* (1916), 9. *Creative Intelligence* (1917), 10. *Lectures at Tokyo Imperial University* (1920), 11. *Reconstruction in Philosophy* (1920), 12. *Human Nature and Conduct* (1922), 13. *Experience and Nature* (1925), 14. *The Public and Its Problem* (1927), 15. *The Quest for Certainty* (1927), 16. *Art as Experience* (1934), 17. *A Common Faith* (1934), 18. *Philosophy and Civilisation* (1934), 19. *Liberalism and Social Action* (1935), 20. *Experience in Education* (1938), 21. *Freedom and Culture* (1939), 22. *Theory of Valuation* (1939), 23. *Problems of Men* (1946), 24. *Knowing and the Known* (1949), 25. *Education Today* (1949), 26. *Interest and Effort in Education* (1953), 27. *Schools of Tomorrow* (1953), 28. *The Child and the Curriculum* (1956), 29. *The School and Society* (1900), 30. *Philosophy of Education* (1958), 31. *Moral Principles in Education* (1959)

Views on Various Aspects of Education

1. *Philosophy of Education:* Dewey's philosophy of education is given various names. 'Experimentalism', 'Functionalism', 'Instrumentalism', 'Operationalism', 'Practicalism', 'Pragmatism' and 'Progressivism'. Of course, his philosophy of education is mostly associated with the term 'Pragmatism'. All these terms indicate the dynamic, ever-changing and performing character of life. Dewey suggested the application of experimental logic. He emphasised that as all experiences cannot be educative, the business of the educator is to select an experience or experiences which would enable the individuals to live creatively, constructively, dynamically and fruitfully in the changing environment.

What is a thing for? What's its use? Action must precede knowledge. Whatever knowledge we possess has resulted from our activities, our efforts to survive. Only that which has been organised into our dispositions so as to enable us to adapt our environment to our needs and to adapt our aims and desires to the situations in which we exist is real knowledge.

2. *Meaning of Education: Education as a Psychological and Social Process:* Dewey does not believe in absolute values. According to Dewey, "Education is the process of re-construction or re-constitution of experience, giving it a more detailed value through the medium of increased social efficiency". Dewey further observed: "What nutrition and reproduction are to

physiological life, education is to social life". He considered education as "the fundamental method of social progress and reform. In sum, I believe that the individual who is to be educated is a social individual and that society is an organic union of individuals. If we eliminate the social factor from the child, we are left only with an abstraction; if we eliminate the individual factor from society, we are left only with an inert and lifeless mass. Education, therefore, must begin with a psychological insight into the child's capacities, interests, and habits. It must be controlled at every point by reference to these same considerations. These powers, interests, and habits must be continually interpretted—we must know what they mean. They must be translated in terms of their social equivalents in terms of what they are capable of in the way of social service".

"I believe that all education proceeds by the participation of the individual in the social consciousness of the race. This process begins unconsciously almost at birth, and is continually shaping the individual's powers, saturating his consciousness, forming his habits, training his ideas, and arousing his feelings and emotions. Through this unconscious education the individual gradually comes to share in the intellectual and moral resources which humanity has succeeded in getting together. He becomes an inheritor of the funded capital of civilisation. The most formal and technical education in the world cannot safely depart from this general process. It can only organise it or differentiate it in some particular direction.

"I believe that the only true education comes through the stimulation of the child's powers by the demands of the social situations in which he finds himself".

3. *Concept of Social Efficiency*: Social efficiency broadly speaking includes three elements of efficient industrial development and the art of living together. A man must learn to be economically self-sufficient and at the same time acquire qualities and values of an enlightened citizen. An individual must be able to earn his livelihood. An individual who is not able to earn his livelihood is a parasite. Education must take into account economic aspect. An individual should be trained to make the best use of national resources. A school was considered as a 'society in miniature'.

Dewey was a firm believer in democratic values. He, therefore, insisted that education should provide suitable opportunities to the students to imbibe democratic values.

4. *Functions of Education*: Dewey explains the functions of education in these words: "It is a common place to say that development of character is the ultimate end of all school work. In general, character means organised capacity of social functioning. It means social interest and responsiveness". He further says: "The function of education is to help the growing of a helpless young animal into a happy, moral and efficient human being".

5. *Child's Place in the Educative Process*: Dewey observes: "Education must begin with a psychological insight into the child's capacities, interests and habits. These must be continually interpreted, we must know what they mean. They must be translated into their social equivalents—into terms of what they are capable of in the way of social service". In this regard he outlined the function of the teacher as "The more a teacher is aware of the past experience of students, of their hopes, desires, chief interests, the better will he understand the forces at work that need to be directed and utilised for the formation of reflective habits".

6. *Curriculum*. The curriculum must grow out of child's interests, experiences, impulses and needs. The curriculum must be child-centred. He stressed that the school subjects should be woven around the child's activities. Lessons should begin with social topics such as food, shelter, modes of communication, speech, reading, drawing, modelling, etc. While laying stress on the needs of the children, Dewey also took into account the needs of the community in which the children live.

Following are the main characteristics and principles of the curriculum:

(i) Curriculum should reflect the social life and social activities. It should have utility.

(ii) It must follow the principle of progressive organisation of knowledge consisting of educative experiences and problems of the learners.

iii) The new experiences and problems should grow out of the old ones.

(iv) The experiences should be flexible and changeable in accordance with the child's interests and should be graded.

7. *Methods of Teaching*: Dewey said: "All learning must come as a by-product of actions and for its own sake". This reveals his concepts of observation, and direct experience. According to him, a child learns through participation in various activities. He advocated 'learning by doing' and 'learning by living'. He recommended the Project Method which is based on problems, activities, experiments and interests of the learners.

Dewey has explained the problem method of teaching in his books: *How We Think* and *Interest and Effort in Education* as "the processes by which the mind of the individual comes into relation with the objective world. Interest and self-activity are the characteristic features". It is a method which deals with the intellectual processes that are antecedent to induction and deduction.

Dewey briefly recommended the following methods of instruction:

(a) Learning by doing.

(b) Learning by integration and correlation.

(c) Learning through productive and creative activities.

8. *Concept of Discipline:* Dewey held that the natural impulses of the child ought to be directed and disciplined through the cooperative activities of the school—"Out of doing things that are to produce results, and out of doing in a social and cooperative way, there is born a discipline of its own kind and type". Dewey believed that the child's activities—intellectual, social, moral and physical—are disciplinary in their effect if they are carried out in cooperation with others.

9. *On the role of the teacher*: The teacher is engaged not simply in the training of individuals, but in the formation of the proper social life. Every teacher should realise the dignity of his calling; that he is a social servant set apart for the maintenance of proper social order and the securing of the right social growth.

In this way the teacher always is the 'prophet of the true God' and the usherer in the true kingdom of God. He also said: "The teacher is a guide and director; he steers the boat, but the energy that propels it must come from those who are learning. The more a teacher is aware of the past experiences of students, of their hopes, desires, chief interests, the better will he understand the forces at work that need to be directed and utilised for the formation of reflective habits".

10. *Concept of Democracy and Democratic Values in Education*: Dewey states that democracy is the political and moral philosophy of education. "If education is equivalent to genuine living, then democracy is the moral foundation of education. The essence of education is the extension of shared areas of meaningful action and this is also the essence of democracy".

The school as the 'democratic society in miniature' should provide for the participation of the students in the activities of the school on the one hand and on the other hand it should realise the significance of the experiences, needs and interests of the child as a personality.

Democracy postulates full freedom of enquiry into social and political problems and solving them. Likewise the schools should promote a spirit of enquiry in educational thinking. Discussion should be freely permitted. The schools should become guardians of academic freedom. Intellectual or moral freedom is the basis of political freedom. These should become living examples of the practices of freedom of enquiry, experimentation and intelligent communication. Excessive heavy routines and rules are not conducive to self and social disciplines.

Dewey advocates that teacher should be provided opportunities to "participate in the formation of the controlling aims, methods and materials of the school of which he is apart".

To sum up. Dewey wants that education should reflect democratic principles and practices in matters of school organisation, selection of activities and experiences and other matters.

Functions of the School: School Related to Social Life

Dewey regarded school as the 'epitome' of life outside, as the 'miniature society' and also the 'lengthened arm of the family'. He said: "The school, now divorced from life, must be re-united with it through activities that will simplify its relations, develop its essential meaning, eliminate its unworthy and obsolescent features, and extend the individual's social environment so that he escapes from the limitations of the group into which he is born".

Dewey sets out the following functions of the school:

1. *Providing a Simplified Environment*: A complex civilisation is too complex to be assimilated in toto. It has to be broken up into portions, and assimilated in a gradual and graded way. The relationships of our present social life are so numerous and so inter-woven that even a child placed in the most favourable position could not readily share in many of the most important of them. The first function of the school, therefore, is to select those features which are fairly fundamental and capable of being responded to by the young.

2. *Eliminating 'the Unworthy Features of the Existing Environment'*: Dewey explains this point: "As a society becomes more enlightened, it realises that it is responsible not to transmit and conserve the whole of its existing achievements but only such as make for a better future society. The school is the chief agency for the accomplishment of this end".

3. *Balancing the Various Elements in the Social Environment*: It is the function of the school to coordinate within the disposition of each individual the diverse influences of the various social environments into which he enters.

That education which does not occur through forms of life, forms that are worth living for their own sake, is always a poor substitute for the genuine reality, and tends to cramp and to deaden.

The school, as an institution, should simplify existing social life; should reduce it, as it were, to an embryonic form. Existing life is so complex that the child cannot be brought into contact with it without either confusion or distraction; he is either overwhelmed by the multiplicity of activities which are going on, so that he loses his own power of orderly reaction, or he is so stimulated by these various activities that his powers are prematurely called into play and he becomes either unduly specialised or else disintegrated.

The social life of the child is the basis of concentration or correlation in all his training or growth: The social life gives the unconscious unity and the background of all his attainments. The subject-matter of the school curriculum should mark a gradual differentiation out of the primitive unconscious unity of social life.

We violate the child's nature and render difficult the best ethical results by introducing the child too abruptly to a number of special studies, of reading, writing, geography, etc. out of relation to this social life.

The true centre of correlation on the school subject is not science, nor literature, nor history, nor geography but the child's own social activities.

The studies represent the possibilities of development inherent in the child's immediate crude experience.

Laboratory School, University of Chicago

Objective: Dewey felt that the changed times demanded that the training of students for a complete living in the society should be provided in the school. For finding out the type of training to be imparted, he carried out his experiments in the school which he established in 1896.

Problems: Following were the main educational problems which Dewey wanted to solve:

1. How to bring the school into closer relation with the home and surrounding life.
2. How to introduce subject-matter in various disciplines like history, science and art to impart a positive value and real significance in child's life.
3. How can instructions in different subjects be carried on with everyday experience and occupation, as the background and be correlated with each other.
4. How individual powers and needs be catered to.

Manual Occupations as the Basis: Dewey introduced the following manual occupations related to everyday life for imparting knowledge of various subjects:

(i) Shop work with wood and tools.
(ii) Cooking work
(iii) Work with textiles (sewing and weaving).

Dewey accorded a central place to occupations and other subjects were treated incidentally as ancillary to practical activities. Dewey observed that the students think out how to make cloth and reinvent the carding frame, tool for spinning and understand the loom. They learn at the same time enough art and science. "Make the construction adequate, make it full, free and flexible, give it a social motive, something to tell and you have a work of art". Likewise, the knowledge of various subjects revolves round such occupations.

Graded Curriculum: Development of interests through

occupations was to take place in a developing sequence in accordance with the mental development of the child. Elementary school life was divided into the following periods.

1. Play Period (4 to 8 years of age).
2. Period of Spontaneous Attention (8 to 12 years of age).
3. Period of Affective Attention (12 years onwards).

In the elementary school, the curriculum is based on the four-fold interest of the child.

a. Interest in conversation and communication.
b. Interest in inquiry.
c. Interest in making things or construction.
d. Interest in artistic expression.

Dewey's Instrumentalism and Experimentalism

Before discussing the various dimensions of instrumentalism, it may be stressed that instrumentalism and experimentalism are complementary and supplementary.

Dewey's instrumentalism implies that education serves as an instrument, *i.e.,* means of achieving the ends of producing a socially efficient individual by providing continuous experiences and integrating knowledge. Education is an instrument of 'catching up' the spirit of the social group to which an individual belongs. Instrumentalism is the name given to pragmatism by Dewey.

Chief Characteristics of Dewey's Instrumentalism

1. *Nature of an Idea*: According to Dewey's instrumentalism, no idea is fixed or permanent or true in itself. The goodness of an idea is tested through experiments. An idea is considered good if it becomes an instrument of controlling a situation. Otherwise it has no significance.

2. *Nature of Knowledge*: According to instrumentalism 'knowledge for the sake of knowledge has no significance'. Only that knowledge is true and useful that enables an individual to adjust himself to his environment. Knowledge is the basis for further experimentation. Knowledge is gradually modified through "continuous reorganisation and reconstruction of experiences and integration of activities".

3. *Nature of Values*: An instrumentalist considers every value relative and subjective. Values are considered useful in the context

of a situation. A value may be more useful in one study and not so useful in another study.

A value has been defined by Dewey as "The value means primarily to prize, to esteem, to appraise, to estimate. It means the act of cherishing something, holding it and also the act of passing judgment upon the nature and amount of values as compared with others".

4. *Order of Values*: It is not possible to determine the order or hierarchy of values. An instrumentalist chooses values according to the task in hand.

5. *Role of the Teacher in Deciding Values*: A teacher chooses values according to particular objective to be achieved.

Major Concerns of an Instrumentalist: An instrumentalist considers that reality is within the experiment. Experiment is the basis to test the truth.

An instrumentalist also considers school as an instrument of achieving the goals of education and this is possible through experiences.

Educational Implications of Instrumentalism

Dewey as an instrumentalist considers education as a dynamic force. For him it is not merely unfolding the latent powers of the child, it is not merely preparation for remote future, but it is rather constant reorganisation or reconstruction of human experiences. Growth is a continuous unending life process and, therefore, it requires a constant reorganisation, reconstruction and integration of experiences and activities. Every human activity should lead to some sort of learning and enrichment of the learner. Every human activity must have an immediate and approximate end. It should lead to present learning or in other words an enrichment of the meaning of the present experience. But this is not enough. Activity and experience should enter into new combinations. They should increase the ability to direct further normal activities and experiences.

Experimentalism

Experimentalism is the key word in Dewey's scientific methodological procedure. According to him, "The heart of the experimental method is determination of the significance of observed things by means of deliberate instruments of modes of interaction".

Dewey is a firm believer in the universal application of the experimental method developed by modern science. Furthermore he stresses the cultivation of the scientific spirit of detachment, impartiality and objectivity.

Dewey's Experimental Philosophy: The new philosophy of education is an experimental philosophy. All experiences cannot be educative. The traditional education gave pupils experiences but not of the right type. The business of the educator is to set a kind of experience which while being agreeable promotes having desirable future experiences. The central problem of an educator based upon experience is to select the kind of present experiences that live fruitfully and creatively in subsequent experiences. The continuity of experience is the philosophy of educative experience. It is held that education is development within, by, and for experience... Education by, of, and for experience... Thus a full integrated personality exists only when successive experiences are integrated. This continuity and interaction provide the measure of the educative significance, and value of an experience.

Experience and Experimental Method: Dewey explains that where there is experience, there is a living being. In the orthodox view, experience is regarded primarily as a knowledge affair. But to eyes not looking through ancient spectacles, it assuredly appears as an affair of the intercourse of living being with its physical and social environment. To learn from experience is to make a backward and forward connection between what we do to things and what we enjoy or suffer from things in consequences.

Three Stages of Activities and Experiences

An educationally important activity passes through three stages.

In the first stage, the child starts his activity in an unregulated manner. Its meaning and significance are not understood. It begins in an impulsive form, *i.e.,* it is blind. It does not know what it is about, that is to say, what are its interactions with other activities. Its consequences are not anticipated.

In the second stage, by doing things constantly, mind gradually grasps the meaning and the activity becomes purposeful. The mind now understands. It can anticipate the consequences also. Results come by intention and not by accident.

In the third stage, activity and experience imparts to the mind the power of subsequent direction and control. The mind can, at this stage, combine old activities and experiences into new patterns to meet novel situations.

Three Types of Activities

1. An activity may be aimless and at random. One does not care what happens. One just lets oneself go and avoids connecting the consequences of one's act. We frown upon such aimless random activity of children. But in fact such activity is due to maladjustment with surroundings.

Children do things under external influence. Children do things because they are asked to do things. They act blindly without having a purpose of their own. Our present day education is confined to this level, resulting in little learning. This state of affairs must be changed.

2. The second type of activity is the positive activity which increases skill to do a particular thing. It has only a limited educative effect. Nevertheless this has a place in Dewey's concept of education.

3. A genuinely educative activity is that which leads to new perception of connections and consequences. Educative experiences are those which help us to meet new situations. So we should keep an eye not only on results but on processes.

"Every continuous experience or activity is educative and all education resides in having such experiences".

True education should, therefore, help reconstruction and reorganisation of experience for future work. It should be both retrospective and prospective. This reconstruction of experience may be both personal and social. The immature child has to "catch up" the spirit of the social group to which he belongs.

The experiences of the young should be shaped according to their future needs. True education is not content with mere production of habits but rather with forming better habits so that the future society is an improvement upon the present one. Unworthy features of our civilisation are to be eliminated by conscious efforts. Education should build up a better and happier world and it is possible only if the process of re-construction and reorganisation of human knowledge on the past experience and activity is constantly carried on.

Basic Elements of Experimentation

1. The problem must be clearly defined.
2. Attempts may be made to review the literature related to the problem.
3. Hypothesis should be formed.
4. Instruments should be clearly selected.
5. All relevant factors which can influence the result should be carefully considered.
6. Data should be collected systematically.
7. Data should be analysed objectively.
8. Conclusions should be reported in clear-cut language.

Role of the Schools: Educational Implications

What should the schools do?

1. The schools should provide greater scope for a rich variety of activities and experiences.
2. The activities should not be merely unrelated and unconscious ones.
3. These activities should be made purposeful.
4. The interest of the learner must be aroused and constant consciousness of the transfer of knowledge to newer situations be maintained.
5. Projects should be organised.
6. Socially useful productive activities should be organised on a large scale.

Essence of John Dewey's Work: Contribution to Education

1. Dewey fused both the psychological and sociological aspects of education.
2. Dewey emphasised democratic values in all dimensions of education.
3. Dewey laid stress on providing rich and varied activities and experiences to students.
4. Dewey's approach to methodology of teaching led to the emergence of the Project Method in education.
5. Dewey advocated that the programmes of the school should be linked with the life of the society. In this regard, he pointed out that the activities should be simplified and that unworthy activities should be discarded.

6. Dewey wanted that the natural interests of the child should be given due attention.
7. Dewey believed in social discipline that could develop through useful activities.
8. Dewey's watchword was social efficiency coupled with individual efficiency.

Evaluation of Dewey's Work

Following points of criticism are usually made:

1. Dewey does not suggest any definite aim of education.
2. Dewey attaches more importance to materialism.
3. Dewey does not accept any truth as something permanent.
4. Dewey puts excessive emphasis on individual differences.
5. Dewey lays too much emphasis on experiences.

Prof. V.P. Verma in *Studies in the Philosophy of Education* (1964) has given the following merits and demerits of Dewey's theory of education.

Merits: (a) It is a 'social' theory of education as opposed to the stress on the isolated self of the individual.

(b) It is a passionate plea for a wide application of the 'experimental' method in education.

(c) It provides the conception of 'democracy' as a social psychological theory of the progressive extension of shared experiences.

Demerits: (a) Dewey's attempt to trace the roots of the dualist approach (two opposed groups of antagonistic interests)—two-fold division of society is a mistake.

(b) Scientific objectivity and veracity may be difficult for being reconciled with democracy, which in practice, means numerical majority.

(c) The neglect of religious education may result in the destruction of the roots of humanistic values and social ethics.

Fredrik Mayor in his '*American Ideas in Education*' has summed up the contribution of John Dewey in these words: "In Dewey the voice of the pioneer, the stirring energies of the reformer, the patient method of the scientist and the faith of the teacher are united in a search for a new education through which man can survive in a chaotic age".

According to Rusk, "In education we cannot but be grateful to Dewey for his great services in challenging the old 'static cold storage ideal of knowledge' and in bringing education more into accord with the activities of present day life".

Regarding the work of Dewey, Irwin Edman (Ed.) in *John Dewey: His Contribution to American Tradition* (1955) has observed: "The breakdown of the violation of school from society, of book learning from vital experience, of the individual from his environment—the extent to which schools and colleges have removed these separations is a measure of the direct impact of refreshing reconstruction of Dewey's thinking".

Prof. Ulich in *History of Educational Thought* has summed up the contribution of John Dewey in these words: "Dewey's work encourages an experimental and scientific attitude. It shows what men can achieve if they rely on their reason and courage instead of clinging to their prejudice".

17
Emile Durkheim
(1858-1917)

Durkheim, a French Social Scientist, is usually considered as the 'Father of Educational Sociology'. The young Durkheim sensed that he had a role to play in the progress of society and that by choosing to be a teacher he could contribute to that progress through education. For a few years, he taught philosophy in secondary schools. In 1887, he became lecturer in Social Science and Pedagogy. In 1902, he took a chair in the Science of Education, later renamed Science of Education and Sociology at Sorbonne in Paris—a post he held until his death in 1917.

Major Works

Durkheim wrote in French but today all his works have been translated into several languages of the world.

1. *The Division of Labour in Society.*
2. *The Rules of Sociological Method.*
3. *Suicide.*
4. *The Elementary Forms of Religious Life.*
5. *Education and Sociology.*
6. *Sociology and Philosophy.*
7. *The Education Morale.*
8. *Pragmatism and Sociology.*

The Function and Meaning of Education

According to Durkheim, "Education is the action exercised by the adult generations over those who are not yet ready for social life. Its purpose is to arouse and develop in the child a certain number of physical, intellectual and moral states which are demanded of him both by the political society as a whole and by the specific environment for which he is particularly destined. Education consists of a methodical socialisation of the young generation":

Components of the School System

Durkheim describes the components of the school system in these words: "Any school system is made up of two kinds of components. On the one hand, there are a whole series of fixed stable arrangements and established methods, in a word, institutions; but at the same time, within the machine thus constituted, there are underlying ideas at work, urging it to change. Seen from the outside, secondary education appears to us as a series of establishments whose physical and moral organisation is fixed; but, seen from another angle, that same organisation harbours aspirations seeking fulfillment. Underlying this fixed, consolidated existence there is a life on the move which, though less visible, is by no means insignificant".

In his series of lectures, Durkheim clearly stated that educational reforms reflect the general context and the way in which the school takes care of emerging needs.

Moral Education

Durkheim attempted to establish that there might very well be a rational basis for a 'moral' and not only 'intellectual' education which derived its authority neither from religion nor from pure ideologies. He was convinced that a rationalist faith and an individual-oriented scheme for action were not separable and that children should therefore be taught to submit voluntarily to the rules of a society that placed the cult of the individual at the heart of its values. Durkheim explained this as: "Moral discipline is not only useful for moral life as such; its action extends beyond that. It plays a significant role in the shaping of character and of the personality in general. Indeed, what is most essential in character is the aptitude to exercise self-control, the faculty of restraint, or, as they say, inhibition that enables us to contain our passions and desires and to call them to order... Discipline is useful, therefore, not only in the interest of society and as an indispensable means without which there would be no regular cooperation, but in the interest of the individual himself. Especially in democratic societies like ours children must be taught this healthy moderation. This is because the conventional barriers, which forcibly curbed desires and ambitions in societies organised differently, have partly fallen away and so only moral discipline is left to exercise this regulatory function".

The Teacher-Pupil Relationship

Durkheim was very emphatic that the outcome of the process of education depends basically on the attitudes of the teacher in relation to pupils. He stressed that to perform his functions effectively, the teacher must have a 'deep sense of his mission' so as to command a specific form of 'respect' from his pupils. He observed: "It is 'through words and gestures' that the 'great moral ideas of his time and of his country', of which he is the exponent, can be transmitted from his own consciousness to that of the child; those words and those gestures must therefore be conceived by the teacher having regard to that very purpose".

Conception of a Class

Durkheim outlined the conception of a class as a teacher-pupil group. He wrote in this regard: "There is a special form of psychology that is of particular importance to the teacher, namely group psychology. A class is in fact a miniature society and must not be conducted as though it were merely a conglomeration of individuals independent from each other. Children in class think, feel and act differently from when they are apart. In a class there will be phenomena of contagion, demoralisation, mutual excitement and healthy effervescence and these must be discerned so that they can be either prevented, countered or used, as the case may be".

Durkheim further wrote: "The teacher must be on the lookout for everything that he may cause all the children in the same class to sense their unity in a common enterprise".

The better the teacher is able to keep the classroom group alive, the more the school will open up to society as a whole, and the more forces there will be to counteract the risk of despotism, a risk proportionality greater the younger the pupils.

School Curriculum

Durkheim's interest in achieving the objective of 'socialisation of the pupil' led him to concern himself with the teaching of these subjects in primary and secondary schools: Literature and arts, mathematics and the natural sciences. He observed, "Our aim must be to make each of our pupils not a complete scientist but a complete reasoning being. We must train rationalists, in other words people who are intent on clear thinking".

Training of Teachers

Durkheim repeatedly insisted that side-by-side and including a 'psychological culture', the subject of sociology must become an integral part of teacher training programme. This subject according to him should help teachers to have a clear idea of their place within the educational system. A grounding in sociology as part of teacher training programme would encourage the teachers to engage in reflection both as individuals and as a group so as to better grasp the meaning of pedagogical practices. They would also go beyond routine and legacy of the past and become aware of social dynamics. Durkheim maintained that this would guide the teachers how to conduct the classroom group, control their own authoritarian attitudes and understand their pupils.

One of the direct consequences of Durkheim's views on pedagogy and teacher training was the introduction of a course in sociology in the curricula of primary-school teacher training colleges in 1920s.

Essence of Educational Thought of Durkheim

In the words of Prof. Jean-Claude Filloux, "The fact that Durkheim in effect inaugurated, under the name 'Sociology of Education', a 'scientific' approach to educational facts as social functions gave rise to an extensive body of literature in several countries dealing with the study of the relations between school and society". (*Source*: 'Emile Durkheim', Jean-Claude Filloux in 'Prospects', Vol. I, 23 (1/2), 1993)

18

A.N. Whitehead

(1861-1974)

Born in Ramsgate, England, A.N. Whitehead, an Englishman, was an educator, mathematician and philosopher. He taught at Cambridge University and London University until 1924 when he joined the faculty of Harvard University in the United States.

Whitehead's writings on mathematics, logic, and the theory of knowledge laid the groundwork for his philosophical classic, *Process and Reality* (1929). This book explains that process and growth are the fundamental ideas which lead us to understand God, nature and our own experiences.

Bertrand Russell was one of his most favourite students.

Publications

1. *Principles of Mathematics* (joint author with Bertrand Russell).
2. *Science and the Modern World.*
3. *Process and Reality.*
4. *Aims of Education.*

Concept of Philosophy

According to Whitehead, there was an intimate relationship between philosophy and environment. He wrote, "The doctrine I am maintaining is that neither physical nature nor life can be understood unless we fuse them together as essential factors in the composition of really real things. There is a unity—of the body and soul—into one person. Philosophy begins in wonder, and at the end when philosophic thought has done its best, the wonder remains".

For Whitehead, the educated man has general culture and expertise in some speciality. His general culture is intellectual, aesthetic and moral. Learning should not just be the storing of inert ideas, or a sharpening of supposed faculties, but should be an active assimilation of general ideas.

These ideas should be tested, applied to life and interrelated as much as possible to give an understanding of the present. To achieve this, not too much should be taught, but it should be taught thoroughly.

Purpose of Education

The students are alive, and the purpose of education is to stimulate and guide their self-development. It follows as a corollary from this premise, that the teachers also should be alive with living thoughts. (Aims of Education p. v)

Education is the acquisition of the art of the utilisation of knowledge. (Aims of Education p. 6)

Culture is activity of thought, and receptiveness to beauty and humane feeling. Scraps of information have nothing to do with it. A merely well informed man is the most useless bore on God's earth. What we should aim at producing is men who possess both culture and expert knowledge in some special direction. (*Ibid*, p. 1).

When one considers in its length and in its breadth the importance of this question of the education of the nation's young, the broken lives, the defeated hopes, the national failures, which result from the frivolous inertia with which it is treated, it is difficult to restrain within oneself a savage rage. In the conditions of modern life the rule is absolute, that the race which does not value trained intelligence is doomed. Not all your heroism, not all your social charm, not all your wit, not all your victories on land or at sea, can move back the finger of fate. (*Ibid*, p. 22).

Concept of Education

It must never be forgotten that education is not a process of packing articles in a trunk. Such a simile is entirely inapplicable. It is, of course, a process completely of its own peculiar genus. Its nearest analogue is the assimilation of food by a living organism: and we all know how necessary to health is palatable food under suitable conditions. (*Ibid*, p. 51).

I do not share in this reverence for knowledge as such. It all depends on who has the knowledge and what he does with it. That knowledge which adds greatly to character is knowledge so handled as to transform every phase of immediate experience. (*Ibid*, p. 49).

The pupils have got to be made to feel that they are studying something, and are not merely executing intellectual minuets. (*Ibid*, p.15).

Knowledge does not keep any better than fish. You may be dealing with knowledge of the old species, with some old truth; but somehow or other it must come to the students, as it were, just drawn out of the sea and with the freshness of its immediate importance. (*Ibid*, p. 147).

Contents or Subject Matter of Education

There is only one subject matter for education, and that is life in all its manifestations. Instead of this single unity, we offer children—Algebra, from which follows Geometry, from which nothing follows; Science, from which nothing follows; History, from which nothing follows; a couple of Languages, never mastered; and lastly, most dreary of all, Literature, represented by plays of Shakespeare, with philological notes and short analyses of plot and character to be in substance committed to memory. (*Ibid*, p. 10).

The sense for style... is an aesthetic sense, based on admiration for the direct attainment of a foreseen end, simply and without waste. Style in art, style in literature, style in science, style in logic, style in practical execution have fundamentally the same aesthetic qualities, namely, attainment and restraint. The love of a subject in itself and for itself, where it is not.

You may not divide the seamless coat of learning. What education has to impart is an intimate sense for the power of ideas, for the beauty of ideas, and for the structure of ideas, together with a particular body of knowledge which has peculiar reference to the life of the being possessing it. (*Ibid*, p. 18).

Characteristics of the National System of Education

There are three main methods which are required in a national system of education, namely, the literary curriculum, the scientific curriculum, the technical curriculum. But each of these curricula should include the other two. What I mean is, that every form of education should give the pupil a technique, a science, an assortment of general ideas and aesthetic appreciation, and that each of these sides of his training should be illuminated by the others. (*Ibid*, p. 75).

Mere literary knowledge is of slight importance. The only thing that matters is, how it is known. The facts related are nothing. Literature only exists to express and develop the imaginative world which is our life, the kingdom which is within us. It follows that the literary side of a technical education should consist in an effort to make the pupils enjoy literature. It does not matter what they know, but the enjoyment is vital. The great English Universities, under whose direct authority school children are examined in plays of Shakespeare, to the certain destruction of their enjoyment, should be prosecuted for soul murder. (*Ibid*, pp. 88-9)

The antithesis between a technical and a liberal education is fallacious. There can be no adequate technical education which is not liberal, and no liberal education which is not technical; that is, no education which does not impart both technique and intellectual vision. In simpler language, education should turn out the pupil with something he knows well and something he can do well. This intimate union of practice and theory aids both. The intellect does not work best in a vacuum. (*Ibid*, p. 74)

1. The Stages of Mental Development

Whitehead mentions the following three stages of mental development:

One: *Romance*. Romance is considered as the first apprehension of vividness and novelty – the child's first contact with knowledge – through observation and experience of the world and objects around him.

Two: *Precision*. Precision is the stage of grammar, language and science, where width of relationships is subordinate to exactness of formulation.

Three: *Generalisation*. Generalisation is the third stage of synthesis.

A return to romance with the advantage of classified ideas and relevant techniques: the final success of precise training... Education should repeat these cycles.

2. Curriculum

Whitehead has advocated the following principles of curriculum construction:

1. Each school must develop its own curriculum.

2. The sequence of subjects should be determined by the readiness, interest and the abilities of the learners.
3. There is no one course of study which gives general culture and another which gives special knowledge.
4. The main ideas to be introduced into the child's education should be a few but important. They may be thrown into every combination possible.
5. The theoretical ideas should always find important applications within student's curriculum.
6. Subjects should not be taught in isolation.
7. The ultimate aim of the curriculum in education should be to acquire Style. Style is the product of careful study and constitutes the morality of mind in the ultimate analysis.

3. Scientific Education

Whitehead considers a scientific education as mainly training in observing natural phenomena and in knowing and deducing laws of the sequence of these phenomena. The firsthand observation is the essence of science and first hand knowledge obtained by observation is the ultimate basis of all branches of science.

4. Technical Education

Technical education is based on scientific knowledge. The other aspects of technical education are its artistic nature, aesthetic appreciation and creativity. Technical training is broader than ultimate specialisation. Technical training should give students the power of adaptation to varying demands suiting the needs of the society. The skills learnt should be flexible.

Technical studies include (1) Biology, (2) Commerce, (3) Chemical Techniques, (4) Geometrical Techniques, (5) Mechanical Techniques, (6) Physical Science, (7) Social Sciences.

For example *Artistic Crafts*, *Carpentry* and *Steel making plastics* all need knowledge of Geometrical Techniques as well as Physics. *Agriculture* requires Biology and Chemical Techniques. *Cooking and Food Catering* require Biology, Physics and Chemistry.

5. Value Education

Value education cannot wait and must be introduced early.

6. Methods of Instruction

1. There is no royal road to learning through generalisations.

Education is a patient process of the mastery of details minute by minute, hour by hour and day by day.

2. Too many subjects should not be taught at a time.
3. What is taught, should be taught thoroughly.
4. Powers of the mind—activity, delicacy, receptivity and responsiveness to stimulus must be utilised in whatever is being taught.
5. In scientific training, 'to prove' is the worth of an idea.
6. Self-development is the ultimate objective of all teaching.
7. The teachers should stimulate the students to think over what is taught and to develop their own individual thought and ideas over and above.
8. Spoon-feeding must be avoided.

7. Technical and Liberal Education

There is no conflict between a liberal education and technical education. Technical education cannot be adequate without liberal education. Likewise there is no liberal education without technical education. True education must strike a harmonious balance between technical education and liberal education.

8. Role of Teachers

Teachers should keep their imagination alive and teach all the subjects with creativity and imagination. They must develop creativeness in the students so that students develop into thinking beings. They must be prepared 'how to learn' by their own efforts.

9. Examinations

Whitehead was a great critic of the prevailing system of examination. His views on examinations were as under:

1. Students should not be subjected to any system of external examinations. He observed, "Uniform external examinations are deadly. They kill the best part of culture. We are dealing with human beings, not with dead matter".
2. No examination system is valid unless every question directly asked of a student is either framed or modified by the actual classroom subject teacher. Whitehead wrote, "No system of external examinations which aims at examining individual scholar can result in anything but educational waste".

3. The best way of examinations consists of frequent assignments and tests designed by their own teachers.

10. Inspection

According to Whitehead, it is the schools and not the students in the classroom who should be inspected.

11. School Autonomy

Whitehead was of the view that each school should issue its own certificates and diplomas to its students, based on its own curriculum.

The schools should be treated as individual units and should maintain their own high standards.

Contribution to Education

Whitehead is the forerunner of several reforms and movements in education. Some of his ideas are quite radical. He does not believe in any curriculum prescribed by any other authority outside the school. In the same way he was in favour of evaluation of the students by their own teacher. His concept of school autonomy is quite revolutionary in nature.

Whitehead advocated self-discipline and self-development through self-effort.

19

T.P. Nunn
(1870-1944)

T.P. Nunn, an individualist educational philosopher inclined towards idealism is considered as one of the great philosophers of England of the 20th Century. He was a Professor of Education at the London University.

Classification of Mind

Nunn has classified the mind in two *Horme* and *Mneme*, according to the process of mind.

Horme is a driver or urge and *Mneme* is a power of conservation.

Horme (Urge)

Horme keeps us active by propelling us to achieve some goal. On account of this urge, we move forward by organising and planning behaviour and experiences for reaching the goal. We shall not be motivated to move forward in the absence of this urge. This power affects our conscious mind as well as controls our unconscious mind. Since the *Horme* controls the unconscious mind, the digestive and respiratory systems of man also begin to help in keeping him active.

Mneme (Power of Concentration)

Mneme remains active in conserving experiences. The impact of the experiences changes although the experiences do not change. Though *Mneme* and memory are closely related, the area of operation of *Mneme* is wider than that of memory. The unchangeable impacts are called as engrains by Nunn and he considers them as hereditary. According to Nunn, all new experiences and ideas are influenced by these engrains.

Environment and Heredity

According to Nunn both *Horne* (environment) and *Mneme* (heredity) play an important role in the development of children.

Individual Aim in Education

According to Nunn, "Nothing good enters into the human world except in and through the free activities of individual men and women, and that education practice must be shaped to accord with that truth". He further said, "Education is the complete development of the individuality of the child so that he can make an original contribution to human life according to the best of his capacity".

Concept of Discipline

Nunn was against external restraints. He wrote, "Discipline consists in the submission of one's impulses and power to regulation which imposes firm control upon chaos and brings efficiency and economy where these would otherwise be ineffectiveness and chaos". He further observed, "The conviction that punishment and the fear of punishment are the natural foundations of school; government is generally being recognised as merely a barbarous superstition".

Publication

Education – Its Data and Principles.

20

Maria Montessori
(1870-1952)

Prominent Pioneer in Child Education: In Dr. Maria Montessori we hear a 'clarion call' to the adult world to pay heed to man in the making.

Dr. Maria Montessori, an Italian, who was a doctor by qualification and profession at the start of her career became one of the greatest pioneers of the education of the very young children of the pre-school age. Before her, very little attention was paid to the care and education of the children in the age group 3 to 6. Incidentally, it may be stated that she was the first woman to become a doctor in Italy.

Maria Montessori was born in Italy on August 31, 1870. While in school, she wanted to become an engineer but after her schooling, she made up her mind to become a doctor of medicine. The doors of the medical colleges were closed for women in those days. How to get admission was the problem before her? She tried a trick and was successful in getting admission. She signed herself as 'M. Montessori when she applied for admission. The authorities could never think that a lady would apply in such a manner. So they admitted her thinking she was a man. This speaks of her ingenuity!

Education of the Mentally Retarded Children

Montessori worked as a professor of Anthropology in the University of Rome from 1900 to 1907. There she was asked to supervise a ward of mentally deficient children. She took a keen interest in their education and made a deep study of their problems. She noted the following points:

1. The dullness of the senses was the reason of the mental deficiency of the children.
2. Marvellous results could be achieved through sense training.

3. If the same method of sense training is used in the education of the normal children, far better results could be achieved.

Origin of Children's House and Development of the Montessori Method

In 1907 Montessori was appointed as a Supervisor of Schools by the Director of Roman Association for Good Building. These schools were located in tenements and catered to the education of children between the ages of 3 to 7 whose parents were mostly at work. These were by and large neglected children. Side by side, her supervisory work, Montessori took interest in studying children and developed a novel method of teaching through sense training. She opened a new school on the basis of her experiment and named it 'Children's House'. Like a true scientist, she observed the real facets of child development.

Training of Teachers: The Government of Italy appointed her inspectress of infant schools in 1922. She began to train teachers for infant schools on the lines of the new method discovered by her. Teachers from several countries from Europe including England came to Italy for training.

Dictatorship of Mussolini and Running Away of Montessori from Italy: Mussolini came to power in Italy; he was a Fascist dictator. He wanted to educate children for war. Montessori, who was an ardent supporter of child's freedom, could not work under such a regime. So she was obliged to run away from there and proceeded to Holland where she founded a school.

Montessori's Work in India: She came to India in 1939 and remained here up to 1946. She spent her time training teachers for small children according to her method in Madras. She again spent sometime in India in 1950-51. She returned to Holland in 1951 and breathed her last there in 1952.

Contact Between Mahatma Gandhi and Maria Montessori

The first meeting between Mahatma Gandhi and Maria Montessori took place when Gandhiji went to London in 1931 to attend the Round Table Conference. At that time Dr. Montessori was holding International Training Courses for Teachers. Common friends brought them together. This meeting inspired Gandhiji, who was also keenly interested in education, to visit Montessori Schools in Rome on his way back. In 1939 when Dr.

Montessori came to India, just after the outbreak of the First World War, Gandhiji sent her a message of welcome. They met and corresponded during the next 10 years.

It is an irony of fate that during the war years, both Gandhiji and Montessori were put under restrictions. Gandhiji expressed sympathy and regret when after Italy's entry into war, restrictions were imposed on Dr. Montessori, considered as enemy alien.

Gandhiji fought for freedom of the country from foreign repression and Montessori for freedom of the child.

Gandhiji wanted to reform the entire system of education especially elementary education whereas Montessori devoted all her energies to reform the system of education at the pre-elementary stage.

Essence of Montessori's Philosophy

"Child is a body which grows and a soul which develops—these two forms physical and psychic, have one eternal front, life itself". It follows then that "we must neither mar nor stifle the mysterious powers which lie within these two forms of growth, but we must await from them the manifestations which we know will succeed one another".

Publications

1. *The Discovery of the Child.*
2. *Education for a New Child.*
3. *To Educate the Human Potential.*
4. *The Secret of Childhood.*
5. *The Child Peace and Education.*
6. *Reconstruction in Education.*
7. *The Absorbent Mind.*
8. *What You Should Know About Your Child?*
9. *Child Training.*
10. *The Montessori Method.*

FEATURES OF EDUCATIONAL THEORY AND PRINCIPLES

Principles of Education

Following are the main principles of Montessori's educational philosophy:

1. *Principle of development from within*: Montessori believed that the source of education of a child is within himself. She observed:

"If any educational act is to be efficacious it will be only that which tends to help towards the complete unfolding of child's individuality. The child has a body which grows and a soul which develops". Education according to Montessori would be such as it helps in the complete unfolding of child's individuality. Suitable environment should be provided so that the child may grow and develop the potentialities that he has within him.

2. *Principles of individual development*: Montessori believes that every child is peculiar to himself and he progresses at his own speed and rate and collective methods of teaching crush his individuality. She treats each child as a separate individual and recommends that he should be helped and guided in a manner that helps him in his proper growth and development. The teacher is concerned with his mental as well as his physiological development. In the words of John Admas, Dr. Montessori "has rung the knell of class teaching".

3. *Principle of auto-education or self-education*: Montessori is of the firm view that self-education or auto-education is the only true education. She advocates that the child should remain undisturbed by adult interference. Accordingly, she has devised the didactic apparatus which attracts the attention of the children, keeps them busy spontaneously, leads them to learn the powers of movements, reading, writing and arithmetic, etc.

4. *Principle of sense training*: Montessori is a firm believer that our senses are the gateways of knowledge and therefore on their training and development depends the acquisition of knowledge throughout life. She points out that the senses are very active between the ages of 3 and 7 and that a lot of learning takes place during this period. She advocates that the sensory training is the key to intellectual development of children.

5. *Principle of freedom and liberty*: Montessori's belief is that there should be no interference in the way of child's growth and development. According to her, the freedom is the birthright of every individual and she advocates the spontaneous development of the child through full liberty. She does not believe in putting restraints as she thinks that these may 'mar or stifle the innate powers of the child'. She says, "The school must permit the free, natural manifestations of the child if he is to be studied in a scientific manner".

6. *Principle of no material rewards and punishments*: Her view is that rewards and punishments are incentives unnatural or forced effort and the development that comes with their help will also be unnatural. She writes, "The jockey offers a piece of sugar to his horse that he may respond to the signs given by the reins, and yet neither of these runs so superbly as the free horse of the plains".

7. *Principle of motor training or muscular training*: Montessori attaches great significance to motor training also as a part of the early education of children.

8. *Principle of no fairy tales*: According to Montessori, the fairy tales tend to confuse children and therefore, she would like to banish them from the school curriculum.

9. *Principle of reverence for the child*: To Madam Montessori "The child was God". Her school was the temple and duty of the temple was the essence of childhood. She further writes: "Today there stands forth one urgent need—the reform of methods in education and instruction, and he who struggles towards this end is struggling for the regeneration of man". The method as suggested by Montessori gives an important place to the child.

10. *Principle of individual teaching*: Individualism is the keynote of Montessori's philosophy of education.

Role and Functions of the Teacher

Case for the Soul of the Child: Madam Montessori assigns a unique role for the teacher whom she calls a 'Directress'. She emphasises that since the soul of the child is pure and very sensitive, it requires her utmost care. Her motto should be "I must diminish to let you grow".

Replacement of the word teacher by directress: She has replaced the world 'teacher' by the word 'directress' and she thinks that the primary duty of the person in authority is to direct and not to teach. She insists that the directress should have an extensive knowledge of psychology and laboratory technique.

Intimate knowledge of the child: The teacher should have an intimate knowledge of the mind and character of each individual. He should keep the physiological records of each child's development: his weight, height and other measurements.

Doctor-cum-scientist-cum-missionary: According to Montessori, the Directress should be partly doctor, partly scientist and completely religious. Like a doctor she should avoid scolding or suppressing the patient in order to avoid worse situations. Like a scientist she should wait patiently for the results and should conduct experiments with her material. Like a religious lady she should be there to serve the child.

Teacher as a gardener: She thinks that a teacher should care for the child like a gardener who cares for the plant so that the natural growth of the child is properly guided and aided in the process of unfolding itself.

Provision of suitable environment: The directress should allow the child to grow according to his own inner law. Her business is to provide for suitable environment. She should provide children with appropriate opportunities to think for themselves.

Moral values: "Virtues and not words are the main qualifications of the directress". She must banish anger which is a great sin and which prevents understanding the child.

Children's House

The first school started by Montessori in 1907 was called a 'Children's House'. It provides all the requirements of a good 'Family House'. It is a house which provides an environment in which each child may develop in the best possible manner. It has several rooms and a garden which is looked after by the children themselves.

Important feature of the Children's House is that children do everything in the House.

A Children's House has many rooms: (1) Study room. (2) Common room. (3) Lunch room. (4) Rest room. (5) Room for mental work. (6) Gymnasium. (7) Bathroom and (8) Laboratory.

The rooms are well-equipped according to the needs of the children and spirit of the Montessori Method. The tables, chairs, etc. are specially made for children. They facilitate movement from one place to another. Sofas of different shapes and long row cup-boards are also provided. The children keep their didactic apparatus in the cup-board and their things in a little drawer. The blackboards are fixed in the walls on which the children draw or paste pictures of different kinds, according to their own interests. The students are provided with flowers, toys, pictures, indoor games, etc. The lunch room contains low tables, chairs, spoons, knives, tumblers, etc. In the drawing room, the children are provided with their own little shelf, where they keep their soap and towel for washing. There is a small garden also which is looked after by the children themselves. Shelters are provided in the garden so that they can enjoy the open air, can play and work there, may take rest or sleep. They may have their lunch there.

The Children's House also contains a paedometer and a weighing machine to keep a record of the height and weight of the students.

Didactic apparatus is used to provide sensory training, motor training and for teaching language and arithmetic.

Exercises provided in Children's House: Following three types of exercises are provided:

One. Exercises in practical life.

Two. Exercises for sense training.

Three. Exercises for teaching language and arithmetic.

Training exercises in Practical Life: Children in the 'Children's House' carry out activities of everyday life. Therefore, Montessori called these exercises 'exercises in practical life. All work in the 'Children's House' is entrusted to the little ones who execute with devotion and accuracy their domestic duties, becoming singularly calm and dignified. The students are required to sweep their rooms, dust and clean the furniture and arrange it as they like. They learn dressing and undressing and washing themselves. They are expected to hang up their clothes tidily. They lay their tables. The children take turns in various household duties and learn by imitation to overcome difficulties in the process. "Enthusiasm and delight, fellow feeling and mutual aid are characteristics of the children learning the jobs". The students learn how to wash their hands. They learn how to use wash-stands with small pitchers and basins. They learn how to use their own soap and towels. They learn how to comb their hair, cut their nails and brush their teeth and other such things.

Motor education: These practical life exercises are considered to be very helpful for motor education. Muscular education takes place with the movements of walking, sitting and holding objects. The care of child's own body, managing the household affairs, gardening and manual work and rhythmic movements provide motor education. Children also learn how to walk in straight lines and to balance themselves properly.

Discipline in Children's House: Discipline comes through an indirect route, by providing activities which are of great interest to children. Every individual is expected to learn how to control himself by his own efforts which is directed towards no external aim but is meant to keep alive that inner flame on which our life depends. Montessori writes, "In truth, the 'good' are those who move forward towards the goodness which has been built up by their own efforts". Such a discipline can never be attained by way of commands, by sermons, by any of the disciplinary methods traditionally known and employed.

Didactic Apparatus

Meaning of Didactic Apparatus

The word 'didactic' means to convey instruction and information (learning) as well as pleasure. In other words, didactic denotes learning with pleasure. The didactic apparatus, therefore, implies that the apparatus (concrete material) is used to educate the young children in such a way that learning becomes joyful.

Principles of Didactic Apparatus

The Didactic Apparatus is intended to translate Montessori's principles of educational philosophy into action. It is based on the following principles:

1. Principle of development of the child from within.
2. Principle of individual differences of children.
3. Principle of auto-education or self-education.
4. Principle of sense training.
5. Principle of motor training.
6. Principle of freedom or liberty.
7. Principle of learning by doing.
8. Principle of self-discipline.
9. Principle of individual teaching.
10. Principle of excluding fairy tales.

Forms of Didactic Apparatus

(1) Didactic Apparatus for Sensory Training

(2) Didactic Apparatus for the Teaching of Language and Arithmetic

Sensory Apparatus: Purpose and Type

Purpose	*Apparatus*
1. For perception of size	1. Series of wooden cylinders varying in height only, in diameter only or in both dimensions; blocks varying in size and rods of varying lengths.
2. For perception of colour	2. Pink cubes, brown prisms, green and alternatively red and blue rods and coloured tablets etc.
3. For perception of form	3. Geometrical insets in metal, wood, a chest of drawers containing plane insets, series of cards on which are pasted geometrical forms in paper.
4. For discrimination in 'Weight'	4. Tablets of wood similar in size but different in weight.
5. For discrimination in 'Touch'.	5. Rectangular tablet with rough and smooth surface etc.
6. For discrimination in 'Sound'.	6. Cylindrical boxes containing different substances.

The didactic apparatus for teaching language and arithmetic:

(a) Two sloping desks and various iron insets.
(b) Cards on which are pasted sandpaper letters.
(c) Two alphabets of coloured cardboard and of different sizes.
(d) A series of cards on which are pasted sandpaper figures (1, 2, 3, etc.)
(e) A series of large cards bearing the same figures in smooth paper for the enumeration of numbers above ten.
(f) Two boxes with small sticks for counting.
(g) The volume of drawings belonging specially to the method, and coloured pencils.
(h) The frames for lacing, buttoning, etc. which are used for motor education of the hand.

Details of the Didactic Apparatus and its Application

1. Three sets of solid insets.
2. Three sets of solids in graduated size, consisting of:
   - (i) Pink cubes,
   - (ii) Brown prisms,
   - (iii) Rods –
     - (a) Coloured green,
     - (b) Coloured alternately red and blue.
3. Various geometric solids (prism, pyramid, sphere, cylinder, cone, etc.)
4. Rectangular boards with rough and smooth surfaces.
5. A collection of various stuffs and materials.
6. Small wooden tables of different weights.
7. Two boxes, each containing sixty-four coloured tablets.
8. A chest of drawers containing plane insets.
9. Three series of cards on which are pasted geometrical forms in paper.
10. A collection of cylindrical closed boxes (sounds).
11. A double series of musical bells: wooden boards on which are painted the lines used in music; small wooden discs for the notes.

In the above apparatus, the child first uses three solid pieces of wood in each of which are inserted a row of ten small cylinders with a small button for handling. In the first piece of wood the cylinders are of the same height but varying in diameter. In the second, the cylinders vary in all dimensions. In the third, the cylinders vary in height but have the same diameter. The child takes out the cylinders, mixes them up and then puts them in their right places. His hands are exercised in handling them, and he learns how to judge their size by making trials. By repeating the process, he succeeds. This exercise trains the sense of sight and teaches the child to note the difference in dimensions. The apparatus is self-corrective, and the child knows when he wants to correct himself.

There is another piece of apparatus consisting of ten wooden cubes, coloured pink. The child builds a tower with these cubes, first laying the largest, and then on the top of it all the other cubes in their order of size. In this way his eyes are trained and he gets an idea of height. Among the apparatus, there is also a small rectangular board, divided into two parts: one rough, the other smooth. Through this the child gets an idea of different surfaces, and learns to appreciate their difference. There are also a series of materials of different kinds: satin, silk, woollen, cotton, coarse and fine cloth. There are two similar pieces of each of the materials of bright and vivid colour. The child mixes up the materials and then finds out and arranges them in pairs. Another striking piece of apparatus is a little box, containing six drawers. When they are opened the child finds six square wooden frames in each. In each frame, there is a large geometrical figure kept in the centre and provided with a small handle. When the geometrical figure is removed, the bottom is found to have exactly the same form. The geometrical figures are arranged in the drawers according to similarity of form, *i.e.,* in one drawer there are six circles decreasing in diameter, in other, six triangles. Another drawer contains various figures such as an oval, ellipse, rhombus and so on. The easy figures are presented first. The child mixes the six figures together and then puts them in their right places. His eye and sense of touch are educated through touching these forms, and recognising their proper shape. This exercise is an indirect but a very good preparation for drawing.

Madame Montessori points out that in training a particular sense, it is better to isolate the sense as far as possible, *i.e.,* to have silence and to blindfold the eyes for some exercises in which the education of the sense of sight is not being given.

Procedure of the use of Material: The use of the material employed involves three stages:

(i) Association of the sensory percept with the name, "This is red".

(ii) Recognition of the object, "Give me the red".

(iii) Recalling the name of the object, "What is this?"

Didactic Exercise for Teaching 3 R's., i.e., Writing, Reading and Arithmetic. After sensory training, children are taught reading, writing and arithmetic. In her system, writing starts before reading. For this purpose she depends upon the psychological principle of 'Transfer of Training'. In her own words: "Preparatory movement could be converted and reduced to a mechanism by means of repeated exercise, not in the work itself, but in that which prepares for it".

Teaching of Writing

The procedure of teaching consists of three steps:

(i) *Recognition of the Forms of Letters*: For this purpose letters of the alphabet are cut in sand-paper and pasted on card-board. The children are asked to pass their finger over these letters. In this way they gradually learn to manipulate a pencil. The same exercise is then practised with closed eyes.

(ii) *Learning of Phonetic Sounds*: While the pupils are tracing out letters, the teacher tells them their sounds, which they are asked to reproduce. This prepares them for reading.

(iii) *Control of Pen*: In the third step, the pupils are asked to place the metal frame on a piece of paper and draw a line round it with a coloured chalk. The same is repeated by placing the metal inset. In this way two figures are produced on the paper. The intervening figure is then filled up with another piece of chalk. While making upward and downward strokes, pupils are not allowed to move their pencil or piece of chalk outside the outline. Thus, they learn the necessary control of pen.

Teaching of Reading

About reading, Montessori says, "Reading is the interpretation of an idea from the written signs and not merely looking at print. Until the child receives a transmission of ideas from the written word, he does not read". Her material for reading consists of slips of paper or cards on which words and phrases are written in bold scripts. The child is given a card, containing the name of a familiar object. He tries to utter the sounds and then repeats them faster and faster. When the child is able to pronounce the word correctly, he is asked to place the card under the object, whose name is written on it. Similarly sentences, describing actions or expressing commands are written on paper or cards.

Evaluation of the Montessori Method and Didactic Apparatus

Merits of Montessori's Educational Thought and Practices

Montessori has ushered in a new era in child education and especially small children of the nursery stage. Her gospel of love, respect and sympathy for the child has been accepted all over the word. The chief merits of the Montessori method are:

1. Scientific base of the method.

2. Individual teaching.
3. Freedom for children.
4. Education through sense training.
5. Unique method of reading and writing.
6. Learning through living.
7. Social values.
8. Reverence for small children.

Limitations of Montessori's Educational Thought and Practice

1. Mechanical and artificial nature of the didactic apparatus.
2. More emphasis on biological aspects and less on psychological.
3. Belief in transfer of training.
4. Neglect of the training of imagination.
5. Lack of suitably trained teachers.
6. Expensive material.
7. Very little scope for correlation and projects.

Contribution to Educational Thoughts and Practices

Madam Montessori has ushered in a new era in child education, especially for small children between the ages of 3 to 6. It is not without reason that a Montessori school has become a household word. Probably there would be no village or city where there is no such school. Attempts are made to manufacture low cost material which is locally available.

To Madam Montessori "The child was God". Her school was the temple and the function of the temple was to provide a pure and virtuous environment. She writes, "Today there stands forth one urgent need. The reform of methods in education and instruction, and he who struggles towards this end is struggling for the regeneration of man".

By founding the Montessori method, Maria Montessori revolutionised the concept of child education. Her impact on educational thought and practices is universal. She has also made an important contribution to the training of teachers for the pre-primary stage. Montessori ranks among the forefront educators who advocate an environment of freedom to children.

Comparison Between Froebel and Montessori

Points of Similarity in the Philosophy and Practices of Education

1. *Philosophy of Education*: Both recognised the need for the growth and development of small children for the well-being of man. Both regarded child as divine and pure.
2. *Education as Development from Within*: Both the educators regard education as the development of the inner nature of the child. They point out that the function of the educator is to draw the inner out.
3. *Congenial Environment*: Both the educators stress the importance of providing a healthy and conducive environment in which the growth of inner nature of the child should take place in a suitable manner.
4. *Reverence and Affection for the Child*: Froebel as well as Montessori have greatly stressed that there should be an environment of love and affection for the child. His personality should be recognised and even worshipped.
5. *Stress on Sense Training*: Both have devised apparatus for training the senses of children.
6. *Self-education*: Both advocate self-education on the part of the child with his own efforts.
7. *Recognition of the Importance of Nursery Education*: Froebel as well as Montessori have given us a method of educating the infants. They have brought about a revolutionary change in the concept of education at the pre-primary stage.

Points of Contrast between Froebel and Montessori

1. *Approach*: Kindergarten is the outcome of the thinking of a philosopher while Montessori Method is the outcome of the thinking of a doctor and a scientist.
2. *Individual vs. Social Basis*: In the Kindergarten, children are encouraged to work in group. On the other hand, individual work is encouraged in the Montessori Method.
3. *Gifts vs. Didactic Apparatus*: While in the Kindergarten, sense training is imparted through gifts, in the Montessori method, Didactic Apparatus is used for the training of senses.
4. *Play-Way vs. Self-Corrective Medium*: The Froebelian system puts more stress on play activities. All lessons are

accompanied by songs, gestures and movements. In the Montessori method, self-corrective apparatus is provided to the child and the same is used in a specific way. There is less opportunity for play.

5. *Manual Activities vs. Daily Life Activities*: Manual activities like gardening, clay modelling, and nature study, etc. are emphasised in the Kindergarten. On the contrary, in the Montessori Method, besides manual activities, daily life activities like cleaning, dusting, sweeping and washing, find an important place and are considered very valuable to students for learning how to take care of themselves.
6. *Imagination vs. Lack of Imagination*: Froebel recommends the use of fairy tales for developing the imagination of the students. In the Montessori method, there is no such place for fairy tales.
7. *Sketchy vs. Detailed System Teaching-Learning*: The Kindergarten system is not a detailed system of teaching 3R's. In the Montessori system, there is a scientific system for this purpose.
8. *Dispensability/Indispensability of the Apparatus*: The Kindergarten method does not require an elaborate material. It can be made use of even without apparatus and other equipment. In the Montessori method, a good deal of equipment is needed for the 'Children's House'. It also needs an elaborate and rather costly apparatus.
9. *Classroom vs. Individual Learning*: In the Kindergarten method, classroom activities and instruction find an important place. By and large, in it, there is a fixed time-table. In the Montessori method, there is too much stress on individual development and learning; social development aspect recedes to the background.
10. *Teacher as a Leader vs. Directress*: In the Kindergarten the teacher is like a leader who guides the children to sing songs and directs their gestures and movements. In the Montessori method, the teacher is called the directress who provides apparatus to the students, watches them from a distance and comes to their assistance when it is needed by them.

21

Bertrand Russell

(1872-1970)

Bertrand Russell of the U.K., was one of the most creative minds of the 20th century. His researches and insights have made valuable contribution not only to the fields of mathematical logic, epistemology, history, political philosophy but also the realm of education. He wrote two important books and several papers and articles on educational theory. He ran in cooperation with his wife a coeducational school for five years.

Russell lost his parents at the age of 3 and was brought up by his grand parents. He was educated at Trinity College, Cambridge and later on worked as Professor in this institution. He published his first book *Principles of Mathematics* in 1903.

In recognition of his scholarship and outstanding works, he was awarded Nobel Prize for literature in 1950.

Publications

Russell's important works are as under:

1. *Principles of Mathematics* (1903)
2. *Principles of Social Reconstruction* (1916)
3. *Introduction to Mathematical Philosophy* (1920)
4. *The ABC of Atoms* (1923)
5. *The ABC of Relatively* (1925)
6. *The Analysis of Matter* (1926)
7. *On Education* (1926)
8. *The Outlines of Philosophy* (1928)
9. *Sceptical Essays* (1928)
10. *Marriage and Morales* (1929)
11. *The Conquest of Happiness* (1930)
12. *The Scientific Outlook* (1931)
13. *Education and the Social Order* (1932)

14. *Freedom and Organisation 1814 to 1914* (1934)
15. *Power: A New Social Analysis* (1939)
16. *An Enquiry into Meaning of Truth* (1940)
17. *A History of Western Philosophy* (1946)
18. *Human Knowledge, Its Scope and Limits* (1948)
19. *Authority and Individual* (1949)
20. *New Hopes for a Changing World* (1951)
21. *The Impact of Science on Society* (1952)

Basic Ideas of the Philosophy of Russell

1. He emphasised the creative aspect of man.
2. He was of the view that the creative instinct of man, if properly developed can bring about the desired satisfaction.
3. He believed in reasoning and wanted to test all existing beliefs on the basis of logic.
4. He was against atomic weapons. He raised his voice against war during First World War (1914-1919) for which he was imprisoned for six months.
5. He was an ardent supporter of human welfare.

Logical Atomism

Russell's philosophy has been called 'Logical Atomism'.

Russell observed, "The reason I call my doctrine logical atomism is because the atoms that I wish to arrive at as the sort of last residue in analysis are logical atoms and not physical atoms". From educational point of view this philosophy of logical atomism is not quite helpful in planning and implementing instructional programmes.

Russell was an eminent mathematician and he developed his theory as a consequence of his deep and penetrating studies in the philosophy of mathematics. In logical analysis, the objects of analysis are concepts and propositions whereas in psychological analysis, we analyse memories, thoughts, emotions and other psychological processes. The main object of logical analysis is to discover the fundamental elements of the universe and from this it follows that logical atomist philosophy postulates the reality of the universe.

Views on Education

1. *Meaning of Education*: In *Education and Social Order*, Russell wrote, "Education is the process of the perfection of the human being". In *Mysticism and Logic*, he observed, "Education is not only the process of the transmission of external information but it aims at the broad cultivation of the mind leading to an awareness of man's place and destiny in the society and the universe".

2. *Aims of Education*. Russell has pointed out the following aims of education:

(1) Education should aid in the acquisition of skills necessary for the provision of the techniques, goods and services which help in making life comfortable.

(2) Science is mainly utilitarian in aim but education has to transcend a merely utilitarian conception. It has to provide for the wise use of leisure by proper cultural growth. Science can be also an element in culture.

(3) Education should aim not only at individual growth but also at the cultivation of the sense of citizenship.

(4) The sense of citizenship should not remain confined merely to the bonds of social coherence in the nation-state but must also teach loyalty to the world government.

3. *Education of the Citizen*: Russell writes, "The education of the individual is to my mind a finer thing than the education of the citizen; but considered politically in relation to the needs of the time, the education of the citizen must ... take the first place".

4. *Psychological Foundations of Education*: Russell insists that only an education in consonance with the conclusions of modern psychology can eliminate anti-social element. Such an education will produce a generation of children who have been trained in the atmosphere of fearless freedom. Education, properly given, can produce a population free from disease and stupidity.

According to Russell, human desires are the product of three factors: (i) Native disposition, (ii) Present circumstances and (iii) Education. It is possible by means of education to change the desires of men so that they may, in future begin to act spontaneously for the realisation of social good.

5. *Character building*: This means the inculcation of the following qualities:

(i) *Vitality*: Vitality increases happiness and develops the capacity of hard work. It depends on physical and mental health. So the school should provide all opportunities for the development of vitality.

(ii) *Courage*: A courageous person does not run away from fearful situations. Of course, in normal situation, as well as fearful situation, he applies his intelligence and resourcefulness. So the teacher must develop elements of courage in his students through education.

(iii) *Sensitiveness*: It is in the nature of children that they take particular interest in praise and hate contempt. Sympathy makes the outlook of the children wider and helps in developing desirable qualities. The teachers should develop this quality.

(iv) *Intelligence*: Intelligence according to Russell is a power which is developed on account of the instinct of curiosity. Thus education should promote curiosity in the children.

Russell points out that training in character should begin even in the first year of the child. A policy of delicate balance between neglect and indulgence should be followed with regard to the infant.

According to Russell, if conducted on right lines, training in character should be complete by the age of six.

6. *Intellectual Virtues*: The techniques of obtaining knowledge are called by Russell 'Intellectual Virtues'. These intellectual virtues include curiosity and open-mindedness which act as antidotes to dogmatism and orthodoxy which stifle the quest for knowledge. He has also emphasised that without patience and industry no intellectual victory can be achieved. Hence these are also included in intellectual virtues. Exactness or the sense of accuracy is also desirable. According to Russell, there are four forms of accuracy—muscular, factual, aesthetic and logical. The sixth intellectual virtue is concentration.

Thus Russell pointed out the following six intellectual virtues:

(i) Curiosity
(ii) Open-mindedness
(iii) Patience
(iv) Industry
(v) Exactness
(vi) Concentration

7. *Principles of Teaching-Learning*: Russell laid stress on the following principles of teaching-learning:

(i) Principle of satisfaction of the curiosity of the child.
(ii) Principle of enquiry.
(iii) Principle of freedom.
(iv) Principle of knowing the child.
(v) Principle of patience.

8. *Concept of Discipline and Freedom*: Russell explained the case for the greatest freedom in a school in *Education and Social Order* as "I found one day in school a boy of medium size ill-treating a small boy". I expostulated (reasoned) but he replied, "The bigs hit me, so I hit the babies". That's fair".

He further wrote, "Children who are forced to eat acquire a loathing for food and children who are forced to learn acquire a loathing for knowledge".

Russell strongly advocates freedom for the child. He states, "The fundamental idea is simple, that the right discipline consists not in external compulsion, but in habits of mind which lead spontaneously to desirable rather than undesirable activities".

Bertrand Russell has explained the harmful consequences of restrictions on children in these words, "The man whose tongue is constricted by laws or taboos against free speech, whose laws are constricted by an ethic which considers jealousy a better thing than affection, whose childhood has been imprisoned in a code of manners, and whose youth has been drilled in cruel orthodoxy, will feel against the world that hampers him with the same rage that is felt by an infant whose arms and legs are held motionless. In this rage he will turn to destruction becoming a revolutionary militarist or persecuting moralist according to temperament and opportunity".

In the words of Russell: "Punishment has a certain very minor place in education, but I doubt whether it need ever be severe".

"When a child persistently interferes with other children or spoils their pleasures, the obvious penalty is banishment".

9. *Love for Children*: Russell has aptly remarked, "Knowledge wielded by love is what the educator needs and what his pupils should require".

Again Russell emphasises love, "The way is clear. Do we love our children enough to take it? Or shall we let them suffer as we have suffered? Shall we let them be twisted and stunted and terrified in youth to be killed afterwards in futile wars which their intelligence was too cowed to prevent? A thousand fears obstruct the road to happiness and freedom. But love can conquer fear, and if we love our children nothing can make us withhold the great gift which it is in our power to bestow".

10. *Three Divisions of Specialisation*: Russell has made the following three broad divisions for specialisation in school.

(a) Classics
(b) Mathematics and Science
(c) Modern Humanities which include modern language, history and literature.

11. *Reconciliation of Individuality and Citizenship*: Russell has challenged the preventions of the organised state in the name of the individual dignity. He is emphatic in pointing out the inadequacies of citizenship as the ideal for education. Russell has pointed out the defects of the educational practices of Japan, of the English and American public schools for their lauding the ideal of citizenship and exalting patriotic fervour. Russell pleads for the reconciliation of the idea of national and world citizenship. In fact he pleaded for a world government for the elimination of wars.

12. *Criticism of Public Schools*: Russell was fundamentally hostile to aristocracy and as such he criticised British Public Schools because they had a very strong oligarchical and aristocratic bias. Russell was also critical as these public schools acted as the production-factories for agents and managers of colonial imperialism.

13. *Education and Religion*: Russell regards church as an infamous thing. He asserted that church was opposed to the extension of literacy because it flourished upon ignorance. Russell regarded religion as a conservative force. Russell opposed religious education as it was not in conformity with scientific knowledge. Religious education tended to instill hypocrisy.

14. *No control of Education by the State*: Russell is opposed to state control of education because one of the purposes of the state, in education, is to produce citizens "who will be convenient" for the state. Russell criticised the system of education in Soviet Russia as it was not oriented to pure intellectual academicism. Knowledge was not the basic goal of the Soviet System of Education.

15. *Role of the Teacher*: Russell states, "It should be the business of the teachers to stand outside the strife of parties and endeavour to instill into the young the habit of impartial enquiry, leading them to judge issue on their merits and to be on their guard against accepting '*ex-parte*' statements at their face value". According to Russell, "The teacher should not be expected to flatter or prejudice either of the mob or of the officials".

16. *Genuine Culture*: Russell writes, "Genuine culture consists in being a citizen of the universe, not only of one or two arbitrary fragments of space and time. It helps men to understand human society as a whole, to estimate wisely the ends that communities should pursue, and to see the present in its relation to past and future. Genuine culture is of great value to those who are to wield power".

Beacon Hill School

It was largely as a result of studying the problems of educating their own children that the Russell decided to start a school on novel and very 'modern' lines. The school was opened at Beacon Hill, near Petersfield, in 1927, with Bertrand Russell as headmaster, Dora Russell as headmistress and about twenty boys and girls between 4 and 11, including their children, as pupils.

The children at Beacon Hill were taught games, but not football, cricket or hockey. All questions they chose to ask were freely and frankly answered. Russell disapproved of punishment, and opposed corporal punishment under any circumstances. "Every time a child is slapped, a complicated turmoil of conflicting passions is aroused". The children were allowed to be rude if they wished, to go where they liked and read what they liked.

But Bertrand Russell has never believed that young children should be left entirely uncontrolled; on the contrary, he considers that they should be encouraged early to realise that they have duties to others and to society, and that learning what is necessary to enable them to play their part in the world is one of these duties. "Some departure from complete liberty is unavoidable if children are to be taught anything". Hence lessons were compulsory at Beacon Hill and so were certain other observances such as cleanliness, punctuality, respect for other people's property, and enough daily routine to give a child a feeling of security.

Russell's Scheme of Education

Stages of Education and Instruction at Each Stage

1.	Nursery Stage/Nursery School	–	Below 5 years of age
2.	Elementary Stage	–	Between 6 to 14 years of age
3.	Secondary/Senior Secondary Stage	–	Between 14 to 18 years of age
4.	University Stage	–	Above 18 years of age

(a) *Nursery School*: Russell strongly advocated nursery education for the children of rich as well as poor families, city and village.

According to Russell, the main function of nursery education is to develop healthy habits in children. The teacher should have a knowledge of psychology and medical science.

(b) *Education at the Elementary Stage (6 to 14 years of age)*: Important suggestions given by Russell are:

One. General education for 8 years.

Two. Reading, writing, dancing, singing, dancing and painting during the first 5 years.

Three. Subjects requiring mental powers to be taught after the age of 7 years.

Four. Science and mathematics to be taught after the age of 12.

Five. Classical language to be taught between 12 and 14 years of age.

(c) *Education at the Secondary and Senior Secondary Stage*: Russell considered education at this stage as a sort of specialisation. He advocates that this stage of education should be for the intelligent children only. He divides curriculum into three groups: (1) Classical Languages, (2) Mathematics and Science, (3) Modern Humanities.

Russell advocates a pleasing environment, full of activities so that children remain active participants in the teaching-learning environment.

(d) *University Education*: Russell wanted to restrict university for those who are really talented and have keen desire to pursue higher education. He advocated admission tests for entrance into higher education. According to Russell, University education has two aims.

1. Preparing men and women for various vocations.
2. Expanding knowledge and research.

Day Schools and Boarding Schools

Russell was an ardent supporter of day schools and boarding schools.

Contribution to Education

1. The most important contribution of Russell as an educational philosopher is his fundamental stress on freedom in education. The concept of freedom championed by Russell is the key to educational progress and advancement.

2. Russell has advocated a profound faith in the transforming power of education. Education according to him, if properly conducted can produce a generation of human beings who have health, generosity, vigour and joy. This hope and faith in the regenerative power of education is immensely satisfying.

3. The quest of Russell for a firm and robust moral character through education may be regarded as his third important contribution to educational thought.

Evaluation of Russell's Contribution to Education

Prof. V.P. Verma in his book *Studies in the Philosophy of Education* has observed that Russell "is important in the history of educational thought because he has had the boldness—although sometimes this boldness has been mistaken specially with regard to problems of religion and sex—to challenge established conventions. He has successfully played the role of a critic. He has made an active and energetic proposal from the intellectual standpoint. This is a very great service to democratic community... His life as well as his writings are inspiration to educationists".

Russell's most important contribution to the field of education has been his plea for the recognition of the rights of the individual. The process of education can benefit from his thought provoking arguments on the need for freedom in education, his concept of an ideal teacher and his emphasis on the concept that education begins from birth.

Russell's view on the concept of freedom and discipline are quite progressive. His advocacy for nursery education is quite justified. As regards higher education, he overemphasises research aspect. His views on restricted higher education based on entrance are quite pragmatic.

22

Isaacs Susan

(1895-1948)

Susan was a pioneer in the area of child education. As a keen and perceptive observer she studied a group of children in school at the Malting House in England. She came to the conclusion that learning should be linked with experience.

As Head of the Child Development at the Institute of Education, University of London, she was involved in various observational studies.

Susan was greatly influenced by the psycho-analysis movement. She observed in this regard, "My own personal study of young children has served only to increase my deep admiration and gratitude for the genius of Freud in being able to penetrate so deeply and so surely to the actual mind of the little child, through the study of the minds of the adults".

Publications

1. *The Nursery Years.*
2. *Social Development in Young Children.*
3. *Children and Parents.*
4. *The Children We Teach.*

In *The Nursery years,* she deals with the daily problems of the children, *viz.,* fear, fantasy, jealousy and rivalry. Other problems dealt with are: companionship, development of skills, value of play in education, thumb sucking, playing kitchen, value of movement etc. She discusses the child's development relationships with the world which surrounds him and suggests guidelines for their solutions.

In *Social Development in Young Children,* she deals with ego-centric attitude among young children, guilt and shame, love and hate, hostility and aggression, social relations and sexuality.

In *Children and Parents,* Susan Isaacs deals with the problems and difficulties of nursery teachers and parents.

23

Paulo Freire

(1922-1977)

Paulo Freire was a Brazilian educator who has made a profound impact not only in the field of education but also in the overall struggle for national development, in the Third World countries. For a while, the methodology he developed was considered such a threat to the established order that he was jailed for sometime and forced to leave Brazil for about twenty years.

Born in 1921 in Recife, the centre of one of the most extreme situations of poverty and underdevelopment in the Third World, he experienced the situation directly. The 'Economic Depression of the 1930s, hit Freire's middle class family, and his studies got disturbed and he fell behind in school. He was so stirred up that he took a vow at the age of eleven that he would dedicate his life to the struggle against hunger so that other children would not have to face the agony he was then experiencing.

He got his Ph.D. in 1959 from the University of Recife and later he worked as Professor of History and Philosophy of Education in the same university.

At Recife University, Freire conducted his experiments with the teaching of illiterates in the city of Recife. This methodology became very popular and began to be used widely. His views were considered such a threat to the old order that Freire was jailed immediately after the military comp in 1964. He spent seventy days in prison and thereafter he was forced to leave the country.

Freire spent five years working with UNESCO and the Children Institute for Agrarian Reform in the programmes of adult education.

Freire acted as a Consultant at Harvard University's School of Education and worked in close association with a number of groups engaged in new educational experiments in rural and urban areas.

He worked as Secretary of Education at Sao Paul city Brazil and Professor at the Pontifical Catholic University of Sao Paulo, PUC/SP.

He served as special consultant to the Office of Education of the World Council of Churches at Geneva.

A member of UNESCO's International Jury, he received honorary degrees from twenty nine universities in Europe and North and South America.

Publications

1. *Cultural Action of Freedom.*
2. *Education. The Practice of Freedom.*
3. *A Pedagogy of Liberation.*
4. *Critical Literacy.*
5. *Education from Critical Consciousness.*
6. *Pedagogy of Home.*
7. *Pedagogy of the Heart.*
8. *Pedagogy in Process.*
9. *The Letters to Guinea-Bissau.*
10. *Learning to Question.*
11. *Pedagogy of the City.*
12. *Education as the Exercise of Freedom.*
13. *Extension or Communication.*
14. *Theory and Practice of Liberation.*
15. *The Importance of the Reading Act.*
16. *Pedagogy of the Oppressed.*
17. *Teachers as Cultural Workers.*
18. *Letters to Cristina.*
19. *Pedagogy of the Freedom.*
20. *A Revealing of the Pedagogy of the Oppressed.*

Some of Freire's books have been translated into over eighteen languages. One of his books *Pedagogy of the Oppressed,* written in 1970 became so popular that within three decades of its publication, over 5,00,000 copies had been sold world-wide.

Education as an Instrument of Liberating the Oppressed

Paul Freire is considered as a representative of the response of a creative mind and sensitive conscience to the enormous misery and suffering of the oppressed. He argues that the ignorance and lethargy of the poor are the direct result of the entire situation created by the economic, social and political domination of a few. By being kept in such a situation, the disadvantaged are kept 'submerged.' He is convinced that in some countries, the oppressors use the system of education to maintain the 'culture of silence', i.e., illiteracy and ignorance, while in others the advance of technology has adversely affected many people. He pleads that through the right kind of education, avoiding authoritarian teacher-pupil models and based on actual experience of students and on continual shared investigation, every human being, no matter how impoverished or illiterate, can develop a new awareness of self which will free him to be more than passive object responding to uncontrollable change.

According to Freire, "A humanizing education is the path through which men and women can become conscious about their presence in the world."

Paul Freire prefaced a method for teaching illiterates that has contributed to awaken them from their traditional lethargy. In the foreword to the book *Pedagogy of the Oppressed* (1970). Richard Shawl has explained this impact as: "In fact, those who, in learning to read and write, come to a new awareness of selfhood and begin to look critically at the social situation in which they find themselves, often take the initiative in acting to transform the society that has denied them the opportunity of participation. Education is once again a subversive force."

Freire is convinced that every human being, no matter how 'ignorant' or 'submerged' in the 'culture of silence' he or she may be, is capable of looking critically at the world in a 'dialogical encounter' with others. The individual provided with right tools for such an encounter can gradually perceive personal and social reality as well as the contradictions in it. He, with this, can become conscious of his or her own perception of that reality and deal critically with it. A peasant can facilitate this process for a neighbour more effectively than a 'teacher' brought from 'outside'. Freire thinks that "People educate each other through the mediation of the world."

Ira Shor, co-author of *A Pedagogy for Liberation* sums up the concept of education as seen by Freire in these words: "Teaching and learning are human experiences with profound social consequences. Education is not reducible to mechanical method of instruction. Learning is not a quantity of information to be memorised. Instead of transferring facts and skills from teacher to students, a Freirean class invites students to think critically about subject-matter, doctrines, the learning process itself, and their society."

In the liberating class-room, suggested by Freire's ideas, teachers pose problems derived from student life, social life, and academic subjects, in a mutually created dialogue.

Goals of Education. Following are the goals of education suggested by Freire:

1. Power Awareness.
2. Critical Literacy.
3. Desocialization.
4. Self-education.

Narration Sickness

Freire informs us that the "Teacher-student relationship at any level, inside or outside the school reveals its fundamentally *narrative character*. This relationship involves subjects (the teacher) and patients, listening objects (the students). The contents, whether values or empirical dimensions of reality tend, in the process of being narrated, to become lifeless and petrified. Education is suffering from narration sickness." The contents of this narration are "detached with reality, disconnected from the totality that engendered them and could give them significance. Words are emptied of their concreteness and become a hollow, alienated and alienating verbosity.". 'Repeating four times four is sixteen' without realizing the significance is merely the 'sensory' of words and not their 'transforming' power. Narration leads the students to memorise mechanically the narrated content.

Oppression of the Parents/Family

Freire points out that cultural invasion inhibits the creativity of the oppressed (invaded) by curbing their expression. Cultural invasion, whether urbane or harsh is always an act of violence against the persons of the invaded culture. According to him all domination involves invasion. The social 'I' of the invaded person is formed in the socio-cultural relations of the social structure. Homes and educational institutions from nurseries to universities are greatly affected by this cultural invasion.

The parent-child relationship in the home usually reflects the cultural condition of the surrounding social structure. The authoritarian cultural conditions penetrate the home as well as the school. The authoritarian, rigid and oppressive cultural environment determines relations between parents and children. The children increasingly view parent and teacher authoritarianism as inimical to their own freedom.

The environment of the home is prolonged in the school.

Here also Freire recommends the dialogical relationships.

Meaning of Educational Practice

Educational practice is not seen as 'extension' but as 'communication'. Extension is negative in nature and communication positive in nature.

Education is not the transfer, or transmission of knowledge or cultures. Nor is it the extension of technical knowledge. It is not the act of depositing reports or facts in the educatee. It is not the perpetuation of the values of a given culture. It is not an attempt to adapt the educatee to the milieu:

"I see education as the practice of freedom above all as a truly gnosiological situation. In the educational process for liberation, educator—educatee and educator—are both cognitive subjects before knowable objects which mediate them.

Placed face to face before themselves they investigate and question themselves. The more they ask questions the more they feel that their curiosity about the object of their knowledge is not decreasing. It only dismisses if it is isolated from human beings and the world."

Diological Method

Freire suggests the following method:

(a) Active, 'dialogical', critical and criticism—stimulating method.

(b) Change in the 'programme' and 'content' of education.

(c) Use of 'techniques' like thematic "breakdown" and "codification" The method based on dialogue is a horizontal relationship between persons.

←— DIALOGUE

A with B = Communication

—→ Intercommunication

Relation of "empathy" between two "poles" who are engaged in joint research.

MATRIX: Loving, humble, hopeful, trusting, critical

Born of a critical matrix, dialogue creates a critical attitude, it is nourished by love, humility hope, faith, and trust. When the two "poles" of the dialogue are thus linked by love, hope and mutual trust, they can join in a critical search for something. Only dialogue truly communicates.

ANTI-DIALOGUE

A Over B = Communique

Relation of "Empathy" is broken

MATRIX: Loveless, arrogant, hopeless, mistrustful, a critical.

Teaching cannot be done from the top down but only from the inside out, by the illiterate himself with the collaboration of the educator.

The programme has the following phases:

Phase 1. Researching the vocabulary of the groups with which one is working.

Phase 2. Selection of generative words from the vocabulary which was studied on the following criteria:

(a) Phonemic richness

(b) Phonetic difficulty

(c) Pragmatic tone, use of words in a given social, cultural and political reality.

Examples of generating words: Housing. Food, Clothing. Health Education.

Phase 3. The creation of the "codification": representation of typical existential situations of the group with which one is working.

Phase 4. The elaboration of agenda to serve as mere aids to the coordinators.

Phase 5. Preparation of cards with the breakdown of the phonemic families which correspond to the generative words. Preparation of slides.

Phase 6. Instructions to the team of coordinators, creation of a new attitude

Phase 7. Decoding by the group with the help of coordination.

Banking Concept of Education

Freire has introduced the new terminology of 'banking' concept in education. He explains this by stating that narration of the teacher turns students into "containers", into "receptacles" to be "filled". Education thus becomes an act of depositing, in which the students are the depositories and the teacher is the depositor. Instead of communicating, the teacher issues communiques and makes deposits which the students patiently receive, memorize and repeat. This is the "banking concept" of education, in which the scope of education allowed to the students extends only as far as receiving, filing and storing the deposits."

Ideology of the Oppressed. According to the banking concept of education, knowledge becomes a gift bestowed by those who regard themselves knowledgeable upon those whom they consider to know nothing. This projection of an absolute ignorance on others by the knowledgeable is a characteristic of the ideology of oppression. It negates education and knowledge as processes of enquiry. The students accept their ignorance like a slave. Freire here makes an interesting point by stating "but unlike the slave, they never discover that they educate the teacher." Education must begin with the solution of the teacher-student contradiction, by reconciling the poles of the contradiction so that both are simultaneously teachers and students.

Following are the chief characteristics of the banking education which lead to several contradictions in the system.

(a) The teacher teaches and the students are taught.
(b) The teacher knows everything and the students know nothing.
(c) The teacher thinks and the students are thought about.
(d) The teacher talks and the students listen – meekly.
(e) The teacher disciplines and the students are disciplined.
(f) The teacher chooses and he enforces his choice, and the students comply.
(g) The teacher acts and the students have the illusion of acting through the action of the teacher.
(h) The teacher chooses the programme content and the students (who are not consulted) adopt it.

(i) The teacher confuses the authority of knowledge with his own professional authority which he sets in opposition to the freedom of the students.

(j) The teacher is the subject of the learning process, while the pupils are mere objects.

The banking system reduces the creative power of the students. This is in the interest of the oppressors.. The oppressors, through their welfare schemes what they call 'humanitarianism' preserve their superiority. The oppressed are termed as 'marginals', incompetent' and 'lazy'.

The banking approach 'dehumanises' the students and adults in place of 'humanizing' them.

Role of Teachers

A Freirean teacher is a problem-poser who asks thought-provoking questions and encourages students to ask their questions. Teachers according to the traditional approach merely 'transfer' their knowledge. In this process, "Education consists in extending 'knowledge' to passive educatees preventing them from experiencing the development of the active, participatory conditions, characteristic of someone who knows. This false conception of education is a basic obstacle to transformation. Education systems based on this conception surround themselves with a "barricade" which inhibits creativity. Therefore, teachers make the process of education a truly 'gnosiological condition'.

"The conception of education which I present centres around the problematization of the human being and the world, not the problematization of the human being isolated from the world, nor the world isolated from the human being."

He further observes: "As we can see, education as a gnosiological condition which unites educator and educatee subjects in the process of knowing, opens for them innumerable and indispensable roads leading to their affirmation as beings of praxis."

Contribution of Freire: Significant Principles and Practices in Education

Freire's views are summarised as under:

1. The teacher must be imbued with a profound trust in the creative power of his students.

2. The teacher should become a partner of the students in his relations with them.

3. In the banking system of education there should be a two-way traffic. The roles of the depositors, the prescribers and the receivers must be exchanged to a great measure.

4. There should be true communication between the teacher and the students. A teacher cannot think for his students. He also cannot impose his thought on them.

5. Authentic thinking—thinking that is concerned with 'reality', does not take place in ivory tower isolation, but only in effective communication.

6. Problem-solving education—responding to the essence of consciousness– intentionally rejects communiques. Problem-solving 'epitomizes' the special characteristic of consciousness.

7. Dialogical relations—The 'teacher-of-the students' and the 'students-of- the-teacher' leads to a situation wherein the teacher is no longer merely the-one-who-teaches, but one who is himself taught in dialogue with the students, who in turn while being taught also teach. They become jointly responsible for a process in which all grow.

8. In the dialogical relations, arguments based on authority are no longer valid. Authority is on the 'side' of freedom, not 'against' it.

9. In the dialogical relations, no one teaches another, nor is anyone self-taught. People teach each other.

10. In the dialogical system, the students are no longer docile listeners. Now they are co-investigators in dialogue with the teacher.

11. In the dialogical system, knowledge does not remain at the 'doxs' (opinion) level but reaches the level of the 'Logos' (reason).

12. Students, as they are increasingly posed with problems relating to themselves in the world and with the world, will feel increasingly challenged and respond to the challenges resulting in development of new understandings.

13. Problem-solving in the dialogical system stimulates creativity and true reflection.

14. The movement of enquiry must be directed towards humanization. The pursuit of humanity cannot unfold in the antagonistic relation between oppressors and oppressed. No one can be authentically human while he prevents others from being so.

15. Dialogue cannot be reduced to the act of one person "depositing ideas" in another, nor can it become a simple exchange of ideas to be "consumed" by the "discussants". It must be meaningful.

16. Dialogue cannot exist without humility.

17. Faith is an '*a priori*' requirement for dialogue.

18. The task of the dialogical teacher in an interdisciplinary team working on the thematic universe is to "represent" the universe to the students not as a lecture but as a problem.

19. Some fundamental themes should be taken up for 'teaching-learning and learning-teaching' in dialogical relations. The themes may be broken up. The thematic breakdown splits the total themes in search of their fundamental nuclei, which are the partial elements.

20. Themes may be printed by means of brief dramatizations, reading and discussion of magazine articles, newspapers, book chapters (beginning with passages) and recorded interviews.

21. Teachers cannot think 'without' the pupils, nor 'for' the pupils but only 'with' the pupils.

Limitations of Freire's Educational Ideas

Freire's ideas are of a rebel and as such they are too revolutionary to be translated into practice in a democratic set-up. Theoretically they appear to be quite sound but functionally they are *Utopian* in nature. Freire has not provided any framework of a workable formal system of education. His ideas do not take into account the financial and organisational aspects of the formal system of education. Of course, his methodology of adult education can be made use of with some modifications.

24

Marshall McLuhan

(1971-1980)

Marshall McLuhan, the author of two famous books namely *Gutenberg Galaxy* and *Understanding Mediatry*, dealing with the role of the media is known for the phrase 'The Medium is the Message'.

Marshall questions print culture and literacy in the electronic era, points out the characteristics of dropouts and suggests strategies for tackling this phenomenon.

According to McLuhan, the mass media are dangerous but can be utilised profitably in education, provided perception and critical awareness are developed in the young. He advises that media should not be allowed to become masters but should be made slaves.

Main Elements of the Educational Philosophy

1. Liberal education is the utmost necessity in the age of automation. Such an education would enable the youth to participate in an imaginative and meaningful way.
2. An educational system in which there is an in-depth approach to learning, a revolution in attitudes between the teacher and the taught, a recognition of the sensibilities is what is urgently needed.
3. Today children gain information and learn more 'outside' than 'inside' the classroom. Information in textbooks becomes out of date as soon as it is published, because it increases hourly and many changes occur in all fields. Reliance, therefore, on printed material alone for information in teaching, is restrictive, apart from being out of date.
4. Knowledge has been compartmentalised. Sheer

specialism results in instruction by "Specialists" who have little or nothing to do with the knowledge in its broad sense. A unified approach to knowledge is the need of the day.

5. The best education is that which develops "Critical awareness".
6. Instead of learning many different subjects, a structured study of learning and knowledge itself, a knowledge of the world and of life itself should be introduced in schools and colleges, in a uniformed form.
7. The close inter-relationship between geographical facts, biological and anthropological studies, sociological and historical evidence and the overlapping between all areas of knowledge should be brought out through all sensory modes in television programmes so planned.
8. Real understanding of what is taught can best be brought about through electronic media which have the power of bringing about an interplay of the senses.
9. A great revolution in teaching-learning can be brought about by a very wide use of Telstar, teaching machines, programmed instruction and television on a massive scale. Teachers should do all they can to utilise these to the greatest extent with relevance to their teaching-learning.
10. Learning should become an exploration and a discovery, a process of play and pleasure.
11. Art should be taught to all pupils at all levels, but not as a separate subject.
12. In order to make education relevant to the students and to prevent them from becoming dropouts, the impersonal and dehumanising environment of education institutions should give way to one which is geared to their needs and problems. Let them move freely in the school to work alone or in groups.

Role of the Teacher in the Electronic Age

The teacher should enlarge his role and attempt to reach out and exert his influence far beyond the walls of the classroom and school. Instead of remaining in an ivory towers, the teacher should come out and exploit the new electronic resources and use them for the benefit of mankind.

The teacher has to be a dedicated and devoted person. The power of human navigation is in the hands of the teachers. They should be able to steer the path towards the survival of the human race.

25

Brief Notes of Various Thinkers

1. Abelard, Peter (1079-1142 AD). A French philosopher and theologian. His philosophy as a practising teacher and scholar is summed up in two aphorisms:

"By doubting we are led to inquire, by inquiring we perceive the truth".

"A doctrine is not to be believed because God has said it, but because we are convinced by reason that it is so".

The university is regarded as his posthumous child. His Cathedral School of Notre Dame, after a generation developed into the '*Universitas*'.

2. Adams, John (1857-1934). Prof. of Education in the University of London. Stressed the claim of psychology in education; known for his dictum: "He (teacher) must know Latin (subject) and he must know John (student)". Important publications: *The Herbartian Psychology Applied to Education* (1897); *The Evolution of Educational Theory* (1912); *Modern Development in Educational Practice* (1922); *Errors in Schools* (1927).

3. Alcuin (735-804). An English scholar. Wrote in his *Grammar*, "The vowels are the souls and the consonants the bodies of the words. Now the soul moves both itself and the body, but the body is immovable apart from the soul. Such then are the consonants without the vowels. They may he written by themselves, but they cannot be uttered, nor have they any power apart from the vowels".

4. Adams, Henry Brooks (1838-1918). American historian. Introduced the seminar method of teaching. Wrote, "A teacher affects eternity; he can never tell where his influence stops".

5. Adams, James Truslow (1878-1949). American historian and philosopher. Wrote, "There are obviously two educations. One should teach us how to make a living, and the other how to live".

6. Aquinas, St. Thomas (1225-1274). Italian philosopher and theologian. Known for his books *De Magistro*—dealing with the role of the teacher and teaching and *The Opusculum De Eruditione*, dealing with the duties of the parents. Wrote, "Teaching is an art and the first rule of art is to follow nature; that one should begin by what is less difficult and then proceed by easy steps to more difficult questions".

7. Arnold, Thomas (1795-1842). English educator. Famous headmaster of the Rugby School in England. Often regarded as the founder of the modern public school system. Developed the perfectorial system.

8. Ascham, Roger (1515-1568). English educator. Tutor of Princess (afterwards Queen) Elizabeth. Wrote, *Schoolmaster*—a treatise on education. Condemned corporal punishment. He separates children into "quick-wit and "hard-wit".

9. Bacon, Francis (1561-1626). English man of letters, philosopher and statesman. Advised scholars to find 'better scientific method'. His *Novugum Organum* is the 'Scientific Declaration of Independence'. Wanted to 'make a small globe of the intellectual world'. Substituted induction for deduction in the study of nature, thus bringing 'sense realisation' in education.

10. Baden-Powell (1857-1941). An army officer. Founder of the Boy Scout Movement in 1907.

11. Bagley, William Chandler (1874-1946). American educator, who preferred to be listed in 'Who's Who as 'teacher', rather than 'educator' or professor; wrote, "The pupil is immature and helpless and he must not be given a long rope with which he may hang himself". Cautioned against regulated freedom and *laissez faire* in discipline.

12. Bain, Alexander (1818-1903). Scottish educator. In 'Education as a Science' shows "How education is concerned with the efforts of the grown-up part of the community to inform the intellect and mould the character of the young". However, excluded physical education, technical education and professional education from the conception of education.

13. Basedow, Johann Heinrich (1724-90). German school reformer. Voluminous writer, wrote; "All our knowledge comes from the senses, and experience of things is our teacher". Authored *Book of Method for Fathers and Mothers of Families and Nations* and *The Elementary Book.*

14. Beecher, Catherine Elizabeth (1800-1878). Pioneer in the movement for higher education of women in the United States. Organised the Women's Association 'to aid in securing to women a liberal education, honourable position and remunerative employment'. Published *The Moral Instructor* (1838); *Religious Training of Children* (1864) and *Women's Profession as Mother and Educator* (1871).

15. Bell, Andrew (1753-1832). An English scholar. While in India, founded the 'monitorial system' of instruction in which senior pupils teach junior pupils.

16. Bode, Boyd H. (1873-1953). American philosopher and educator. Contended that the 'the purpose of sound education is to emancipate the pupil from dependence on immediate interest. Claimed that 'Child-centred' method had become a cult selling up false 'absolutes'. Published *Progressive Education at the Crossroads.*

17. Conant, James Bryant (1893-1978). American diplomat, educator and scientist. Advocated that the Universities must rely upon experimental spirit. Recommended guidance facilities in School. Published, *The American High School Today; Education and Liberty; On Understanding Science and Modem Man.*

18. Confucius (551 B.C.-478 B.C.). Chinese philosopher, a born teacher and lover of morals. He said, "Learning without thought is labour lost, thought without learning is perilous". Wrote *Spring and Autumn* which was studied for several centuries by Chinese boys in their homes or schools.

19. Cunningham, W.I. (1885-1961). American educator, viewed knowledge as a divine instrument which leads to the knowledge of the Spiritual Kingdom. Maintained that "Knowledge of God is the beginning and end of education'. It (curriculum) is a tool in the hands of the artist (the teacher) to mould his material (the pupil) in accordance with his ideal in his studio (the school)". Publications *Pivotal Problems of Education; General Education* and *The Liberal College.*

20. Defoe (1659-1731). English journalist and novelist, author of the famous work *Robinson Crusoe*. Advocated in his *Essay upon Projects* (1697), the establishing of academics. This book led Benjamin Franklin (1706-1709) to the founding of the Academy and Charity School of Philadelphia.

21. De Garmo, Charles (1819-1934). American educator. Author of *Principles of Secondary Education* in two volumes in 1907 and 1908.

22. Dewey, John (1859-1952). See Chapter 22.

23. Diderot, Denis (1713-1784). French educator and philosopher. The first to say that the blind could be taught through the sense of touch. Author of the monumental work *Dictionnaire Encyclopedique* (1750-72) in 28 volumes and *Plan of a University* (1776).

24. Eliot, Charles William (1834-1926). American educator, prolific writer, leader of college and uniform reform. President of the Harvard University for 40 years. Published *Educational Reforms* (1898) and *University Administration* (1908).

25. Emerson, Ralph Waldo (1803-1882), American educator, essayist, moralist and poet, stated the role of education as "In order to control the minds of the people education should be one part words, one part worship, and one part work". Observed, "The secret of education lies in respecting the child". His ideas found in his *New England Reformers* and *Culture and Education*. Author of the famous quote:

"Not gold, but only men can make
A people great and strong..."

26. Erasmus, Desiderious (1466-1536). French educator and one of the greatest humanists of the Renaissance. Advocated a higher standard of qualifications and proper selection of teachers.

27. Fichte, Johann Gottlieb (1762-1814). German educator and philosopher. Pleaded for same education for both the sexes. Wrote *The Vocation of the Scholar; The Nature of the Scholar* and *The Address to the German Nation*.

28. Franklin, Benjamin (1706-1790). American author, educator, inventor, publisher, scientist and statesman. Founder of the first American circulating library (1731). Provided for a wide curriculum including practical and vocational activities in his academy. Wrote, "It is, therefore, proposed that they learn those things that are likely to be most useful and most ornamental". Publications: *Proposals relating to the Education of the Youth* (1749). *An Idea of the English School* (1750).

29. Gesell, Arnold (1880-1961). An American educator and psychologist. Famous for his contribution to child development, especially at the pre-primary stage. Earned his Ph.D. from Clark University (1906) and M.D. from Yale University (1915). Director Clinic of Child Development (1911-1948), was among the first to study human development from birth through adolescence. Worked with pre-school children and later extended it to ages 5 to 10 and 10 to 16. During 1940s and 1950s, was regarded as America's fore most authority on child rearing and development. Developed series of norms of infant and child behaviour. Publications: *'An Atlas of Infant Behaviour'* (1934), *'Infant and Child in the Culture of To-day'* (1943, *'The Child from 5 to 10'* (1946) and *'Youth: The Years from Ten to Sixteen'* (1956).

30. Grant, Charles (1746-1823). An English Officer in India, advocated English education in India. Chairman of the Board of Directors of the East India Company. Observed, "The true cure of darkness is the introduction of light. The Hindus err because they are ignorant... and it is perfectly in order, by degrees, to impart the Hindus of our language". Believed that "the acquisition of knowledge in English literature, philosophy and religion would silently, undermine the fabric of error".

31. Grundtvig, Nikolai Frederik Severin (1783-1872). Danish educator, historian, poet, statesman and founder of the 'Folk High Schools'. The 'Folk High School' is Denmark's most important contribution to adult education in the world.

32. Herbart, Johann Friedrich (1776-1841). German educator and philosopher, came into contact with great thinkers like Goethe, Schipper and Fichte, Met Pestalozzi when he was still teaching at an elementary school; occupied the most distinguished chair of philosophy at the University of Konigsburg in East Prussia; was against faulty psychology; advocated that human mind is one harmonious whole and not a confused mixture of many faculties; popularised terms like interest, apperception (mental process of understanding in terms of previous experience), circle of thought, concentration, correlation, culture, best known for his 'Herbartian Steps': (i) Preparation or Introduction or Motivation, (ii) Presentation, (iii) Comparison or Association, and (iv) Generalisation and Application. Publications: *'Aesthetic Presentation of the World as the Main Function of Education'* (1804); *'Critical Point of View of the Pestalozzian Method of Education'* (1804); *'Relation of School in Life'* (1818) and *'Encyclopedia of Philosophy'* (1831).

33. Huxley, Thomas (1828-1895). He was an English scientist, social reformer and educational thinker. He did much to popularise scientific educational thought. He showed great interest in questions of education.

His concept of education may be described as: "The man, I think, has liberal education whose intellect is clear, whose passions are trained, who has learnt to love beauty, whether of nature or of art, to hate all vileness and to respect others as himself".

About the prevailing system of education, he observed, the stock example of solid stupidity' of the 19th century. He vehemently criticised the classical education which in no way helped the youth of England.

His main ideas on educational reforms are as under:

1. Elements of physical science should be taught first in schools.
2. Physical training and drill should form part of regular school work.
3. Drawing and music should be included in every school course.
4. State should provide compulsory elementary education, and beyond that an individual should be left to himself to rise through his own innate capacity and efforts.

34. James, Wilnam (1842-1910): American educator and psychologist. Believed 'The great thing in all education is to make the nervous system our ally instead of our enemies'. Propounder of 'James-Lange Theory of Emotions' (1885). Published *The Principles of Psychology* (1890) and *Talks to Teaches* (1899).

35. Keller, Helen Adams (1880-1968). American educator, a pioneer in deaf education. Became deaf and blind at the age of 19.

Wrote: *The Story of My Life* (1902), *The World I Live On* (1908) and *Mid Stream* (1930).

36. Kerschensteiner, George (1854-1932). German educator. Distinguished three aspects of education—the axiological, the psychological and the teleological. Publication *Theorieder Bildung* (Theory of Education).

37. Kilpatrick, William Heard (1871-1965). American educator, popular lecturer and writer. Gave a concrete shape to the Project Method. Publications: *The Montessori System Examined* (1914), *Foundations of Method* (1925), *Education for a Changing Civilisation* (1926), *Education and the Social Crisis* (1932), *Remaking the Curriculum* (1936) and *Philosophy of Education'* (1951).

38. Lane, Homer Tyrrell (1876-1925). British educator and a great champion of self-government in schools. Founded the 'Little Commonwealth', a reformatory school on a Dorest farm in 1912. Put his ideas into practice in this school. Wrote, "Faults are not corrected by, but brought about by, suppression in childhood. The free a child is, the more it be considerate and social, the more its chief interests will be progressive, the more its fundamental instincts will have valuable social status". Publication: *Talks To Parents and Teachers.*

39. Locke, John (1632-1704). English educator and philosopher. He was concerned primarily with the question of how the mind acquires knowledge, and he emphatically said, "To this I answer, in one word, from 'Experience'. In that all our knowledge is founded; fully recognised". Stressed that the business of a teacher was 'to raise in his pupil a love and esteem of knowledge, rather than to teach all that was knowledge'. Wrote *An Essay Concerning Human Understanding* and *Thoughts on Education.*

40. Macaulay, Thomas Babington (1800-1859). English essayist, historian, politician and Law Member of Governor General Lord William Bentinck. Known for his *Minutes on Education* (1835). Founder of the English system of Education in India. Chairman of the Committee of Public Instruction, made very derogatory remarks about oriental learning. Wrote, "A single shelf of a good European literature was worth the Whole Native literature of India and Arabian... False history, false astronomy, false medicine... false religion". Author of monumental work of five volumes of *History of England.*

41. Makarenko, Anton Semyonnovich (1888-1939). Russian educator. Believed that educational failures result from "poor preparedness as a teacher, an insufficient mastery of teaching techniques and a poor state of his nerves as well as desperation". He further observed, "Win over a child's soul, make him your ally, involve him in collective life".

42. McMillan, Margaret (1860-1931). Known for her contribution to nursery education (along with her sister Rachel McMillan and popularly called McMillan sisters). Lost father at the age of 5 and mother at 17. Born in USA but settled in UK. Concentrated on improving the physical and welfare of the slum children. Carried out the first medical inspection of elementary school children at Bradford in England. Began a campaign to improve the health of children and pleaded that local authorities should install bathrooms, improve ventilation and supply free school meals in 1988, began teaching working class children. Two sisters led a vigorous campaign for school meals and in 1906, the House of Commons in England (Lok Sabha) passed the 1906 Provision of School Meals Act. In 1908, opened the country's first school clinic in Bow. In 1910, another school clinic was opened at Deptford. The clinic provided dental care, surgical aid and lessons in breathing and posture. The sisters also established a night camp where slum children could wash and wear clean night clothes. The two sisters created the first nursery school in London in 1911.

In 1914, both the sisters started an Open-Air Nursery School and Training Centre in Peckham. Margaret opened in 1830 at Deptford, a college to train nurses and teachers. Also, supported the campaign for 'Universal Suffrage' in England. Wrote: '*Child Labour and Half the Time System*' (1896); '*Early Childhood*' (1900); '*Education through the Imagination*' (1904); '*The Economic Aspects of Child Labour and Education*' (1905); '*The Child and the State*' (1911).

43. McMillan, Rachel (1860-1917). (See above also.) After 1888, both the sisters remained together for most of the rest of their lives. Wrote: '*The Nursery School*' (1919) and '*Nursery Schools: A Practical Handbook*' (1920). Both placed high value on creativity and play in nursery programme.

44. Newman, Cardinal John Henry (1801-1890). English Educator. Wrote, "A habit of mind is formed which lasts through life, of which the attributes are freedom, equitableness, calmness, moderation and wisdom; or what is former discourse, I have ventured to call a philosophical habit". Delivered a series of lectures in 1852 on 'Idea of a University'.

45. Parker, Francis Wayland (1837-1902). American educational reformer, known for his *Doctrine of Concentration*: "The doctrine of concentration is itself a science of education that will absorb the attention of thoughtful teachers for centuries".

46. Parkhurst, Helen (1887-1937). American educator, author of the novel Dalton Plan or Contract Plan in the School System of Dalton, Massachusetts. Publication: *Education on the Dalton Plan* (1922).

47. Parsons, Frank (1854-1908). American educator, pioneer in the guidance movement. Organised the Boston Vocational Bureau. Author of *Our Country's Needs* (1894) and *Choosing a Vocation*.

48. Piaget, Jean (1896-1980). A Swiss educator and a naturalist and biologist by training. Worked as a Professor of Child Psychology at the University of Geneva. Began his study of child development with the careful observation of his own three children. For over 50 years, observed, interviewed and tested children of all ages. Implications of his 'Theory of Cognitive Development' for early childhood are: (i) young children learn best through direct encounter with the environment than through formal education. (ii) play and activity should be the medium of early childhood education. (iii) the emphasis should be on giving children first hand experiences with objects. (iv) they should be encouraged to observe, describe, manipulate and experiment with them so as to develop clear and sound concepts. Publications:

1. *The Language of Thought of the Child* (1923).
2. *Judgement and Reasoning of the Child* (1924).
3. *The Child's Conception of the Physical World* (1932).
4. *The Moral Judgement of the Child* (1937).
5. *The Origin of Intelligence in the Child* (1937).
6. *The Child's Conception of Number* (1941).
7. *The Child's Conception of Physical Quantities* (1942).

8. *Play Dreams and Imitations in Childhood* (1945).
9. *The Child's Conception of Time* (1946).
10. *The Child's Conception of Movement and Speed* (1946).
11. *The Construction of Reality in the Child* (1947).
12. *The Child's Conception of Space* (1948).
13. *The Psychology of Intelligence* (1950).
14. *Logic and Psychology* (1953).
15. *The Construction of Reality in the Child* (1954).
16. *The Strategy of Genes* (1957).
17. *The Growth of Logical Thinking from Childhood to Adolescene* (1958).
18. *The Child's Conception of Geometry*.
19. *The Early Growth of Logic in the Child* (1964).
20. *Mental Imagery in the Child* (1969).
21. *The Mechanism of Perception* (1969).
22. *The Psychology of the Child* (1969).
23. *Science of Education and the Psychology of the Child* (1969).
24. *The Origin of the Idea of Chance in Children* (1975).
25. *The Grasp of Consciousness*.

49. Quintillion (38-86 A.D.). Roman teacher, lawyer, orator and senator. His ideas on education of children are as valid to-day as they were about nineteen centuries back. Education must begin at an early age, seventh year is the time of definite instructions. Whipping is unseemly. Respect for the individuality of the pupil by the teacher. Character is the end of education. Wrote *Institutes of Oratory*.

50. Ramus, Petrus (1515-1572). French educational reformer and humanist. Principal of the College of Presales. Held that the selection of subject matter should be based on the observation of nature and the arrangement of subject matter should be based on the law of truth, law of justice and the law of wisdom. Wrote 62 works covering subjects like grammar, rhetoric, dialectic mathematics and physics. *Recommendations for the Reformation of the University* (1562), one of his unique books.

51. Ratke, Wolfgang (1571-1635). German educator and one of the pioneers of the modem pedagogy. Initiated the search for the 'Method of Nature'. Advocated the method of teaching of one thing at a time, everything to be often repeated, no rote, learning things first and explanations afterwards.

52. Richter, Johann Paul Friedrich (1763-1825. German educator, humanist and prolific writer. Criticised Rousseau's Emile as a negative scheme. Pleaded for a joyous freedom in the early life of a child, underlined the educative functions of play games, dancing, music and fairy tales. Authored *Levana* (Doctrine of Education) in 1807.

53. Runkie, John Daniel (1822-1902). American educator and leader in the movement for the introduction of manual training in schools. President Massachusetts Institute (1870-1878). Publications: *Manual Elements in Education.*

54. Ruskin, John (1819-1900). English educator, social reformer and writer. Advocated manual training and craftsmanship. Gandhiji greatly influenced by his book *Unto the Last* containing outlines of his proposals for State Schools. *Time and Tide* contains letters on the general subject of education. Sesame and Lilies illustrates the place of literature in education.

55. Sadler, Michael (1861-1943). British educator and Vice-Chancellor of the University of Leeds. Headed the Calcutta University Commission in 1917. Report known as Sadler Report—a great document in the history of Indian education.

56. Sampson, George (1852-1950). British educator who coined the phrase 'Every teacher is a teacher of English'. Publication: '*English for the English*' (1921).

57. Sanderson, Frederick William (1857-1922). English educator and H.G. Well's 'great school teacher'. Said, "Education must be fitted to the boy, not the boy to education".

58. Santayana (1863-1952). American educator, critic, philosopher, poet and writer. Left America and made Europe his home. Rejected the idea that all are equal in education. Believed in a natural aristocracy of talent. Held, "A child educated only at school is an uneducated child".

59. Schiller, Friedrich (1759-1815). German educator, historian, philosopher and poet. Viewed education as a process of emotional development. Authored *Aesthetic Education of Man; On the Sublime; On the Necessary Limits in the Use of Beautiful Forms.*

60. Thring, Edward (1821-1887). English educator and famous headmaster of Uppingham School. Believed that 'everybody can do something good'. Insisted upon individual attention to the bright and dull student alike. Instituted the first gymnasium in any public school in England. Attached great importance to music. Publications: *Education and School* (1864); *Theory and Practice of Teaching* (1883); *Thoughts on Life Sciences* (1869).

61. Tolstoy, Count Leo Nikolayevich (1828-1910). Russian educator and laureate. Influenced Gandhiji. Persistent advocate of progressive ideas. Devoted much time in organising village schools. Edited an educational magazine in which explained his ideal of free education and described his teaching methods. His idea was not to force anything on the child; every pupil was free to come to school; free to sit where he liked; free to learn only when he liked and free to criticise or suggest. Freedom as the keynote of all his educational efforts. Publications: *Twenty three Tales; The Teaching of Jesus; On Popular Education.*